# Library Services in Electronic Environment

# Library Services in Electronic Environment

## Changes Challenges Issues and Strategies

**Dr. Tariq Ashraf**

**Kaveri Books**

**New Delhi - 110 002**

Title: Library Services in Electronic Environment: Changes, Challenges, Issues and Strategies

Author: Dr. Tariq Ashraf



First Published in 2004
Edition 2025

ISBN-10: 81-7479-065-9
ISBN-13: 978-81-7479-065-1

Price Rs. 850.00



*Published by*

**Kaveri Books**

4832/24, Ansari Road
New Delhi-110002 (India)

Tel: 011- 47072321
E-mail : info@kaveribooks.com
kaveribooks@gmail.com
Website: www.kaveribooks.com

**PRINTED IN INDIA**

# Contents

# Acknowledgement

I am thankful to all those organizations, institutions, associations and professionals who have helped me during the course of last one decade in contributing, presenting and publishing the research papers contained in this book. I am particularly indebted to Institute for Integrated Learning in Management [IILM] for providing me the stimulating environment support and infrastructure for practising and applying several of the applications and modules discussed and detailed in the book while working there during the course of last 8 years. My very special and sincere thanks to Mrs. Malvika Rai, Chairperson of IILM who always supported and encouraged research and its application. I am also thankful to Dr. Irfan A. Rizvi, Director of the Institute for his keen interest shown in the publication and many suggestions to improve its contents and quality.

I also take this opportunity to thank all the current and former faculty members of the Library School in Delhi University where I studied Library & Information Science. I am also thankful to my friends in the profession who have always been generous to me and stood by me in my moments of reckoning. I express my heartfelt thanks to all my colleagues at IILM for their bounteous words of encouragement and good wishes.

My thanks are also due to Prof. (Mrs.) Sue O' Neil Johnson, Chairperson, ASSIST-SIG III for facilitating my participation in the annual conference of American Society For Information Science & Technology held at Los Angles in October 2003.

I would be failing in my duty if I do not thank my publisher Mr. Rakesh Goel of M/s Kaveri Books for changing his schedule to accommodate mine and giving his time freely which made publishing of the book possible in a short time.

— ***Dr. Tariq Ashraf***

# Introduction

The collection and interpretation of data, accumulation of experience, knowledge and transmission and exchange of information have been some of the main activities of mankind during millennia. Human information processing activities have been integrated with tools for external information storage and transmission - symbols, languages, pictures, writing and printing. Social information processing is improving in line with the development of society. Several decades ago the development of computer and communications technologies created conditions for technical information processing. The main advantage of technical processing was much more powerful action in terms of speed and amount of processed data.

The amazing technological advancements have opened new horizons for information creation, duplication, storage, access, distribution, and presentation. The pace at which information sources are being produced and converted into electronic form is marvellous. Digitisation of information is resulting in access to an unbelievable volume of information. Treasures of the human intellect previously hidden from the masses, stored under tight security and accessible to only limited privileged scholars, are now accessible to every citizen.

As information becomes an indispensable resource and commodity in the "Information Era," providing information services is of paramount importance to all types of organizations. The cost of providing effective information services is on the rise in parallel with the increasing role that information plays in day-to-day activities of organizations. Yet, librarians are faced with the challenge of providing better services with shrinking budgets.

Electronic resources are now recognized as being of great importance to even small academic and public libraries and they are consuming an ever increasing share of library budgets, often to the detriment of monographic acquisitions. CD-ROMs, local area networks, computer equipment, online resources, the Internet, and other remote databases all provide libraries with vast resources for their user populations. In addition to the benefits of additional access, the information explosion has also produced a considerable amount of confusion on the part of library users and librarians.

As access to electronic information services becomes more widespread, libraries are beginning to lose their monopolies, particularly as far as aggregation and access are concerned. They do however retain strengths in traditional expertise of selecting, organising, and creating access tools for information are just as necessary in the electronic environment especially with fewer barriers to publication and worldwide access. Libraries also continue to play a role both in terms of branding and authority, and in the procurement of information

To provide information for the aforementioned programs and purposes libraries must change their traditional style of work according to contemporary demands. All the stages of information services have to take place in any research library — collection, processing, storage, effective searching and supplying users with qualitative information in the form they need and wherever and whenever they need it. The provision of various information services and creation of information sources has become a complex task. Electronic information technologies are widely introduced for information supply today. They ensure formerly unachievable possibilities, first of all for information browsing and search. At the same time, printed books and journals have some advantages and attractiveness too. It is necessary to specify the role and tasks of each technology in the overall information assimilation process (search-delivery-studying) to find the optimum balance of functions between both technologies. Today's optimum will not be final as various changes will take place in the future too. The optimum balance is different in various libraries because of the different needs and approaches of patrons. The Concept envisages the realization of qualitative information supply by the integrated use of both printed and electronic technologies.

Fortunately, the developments in information technology (IT) create new opportunities for librarians. For instance, librarians can now provide access to networked information sources that their libraries do not even own. They need to weigh the virtues of new approaches such as "access versus ownership." They try to cater to ever-increasing information needs of their clientele through various networks such as the Internet. Interlibrary cooperation and coordination of resource sharing is also facilitated in the network environment as it is easier for libraries to form consortia and share electronic information resources.The proliferation of electronic information services and products, and increasing availability of information processing, storage and communication technologies in libraries facilitated the sharing of resources and engendered new cooperative schemes. Moreover, librarians increasingly feel that they must cooperate to reap the benefits of economics of scale. In traditional resource sharing schemes, libraries possessing the physical materials tend to benefit more from the cooperative collection development efforts. However, the availability of networked information resources encouraged libraries to streamline their cooperative collection development efforts. Possessing electronic information resources does not prohibit other libraries' access to information. This has facilitated cooperative collection development efforts and further encouraged libraries to set up library consortia to provide more and varied electronic resources through the networks and to increase their bargaining power with publishers of electronic information resources.

The amount of information has increased in line with the general development of science and technology. It is impossible at present to acquire all of the potentially necessary information sources. Therefore a strategy of the virtual library should be widely developed in addition to very careful management of acquisition policy. In particular, it concerns small countries where varied information is necessary, but only a few people work in each field and finances would be ineffectively expended. As a result, a traditional complex method of information assimilation, direct examination of documents, selection of necessary materials and their subsequent study, has become ineffective. The Concept proposes complete separation of both components of information assimilation - information search and its study - and choice of optimum technologies for each of them.

In addition to traditional library services, creation and brokerage of value-added information should be developed, such as information searches on demand, active consulting and reference services, creation of printed and electronic information sources, participation in research and technological projects, brokerage of advanced information products and services, etc. All necessary preconditions for such activities exist in libraries - huge amounts of collected documents, global access to printed documents and electronic information sources and highly skilled information professionals. All these applications and services are not separate items. They should be developed as an integrated information system and as a substantial component of the general strategy of development of the library, with the strict precondition to achieve set goals.

Librarians today are grappling with the issues of which electronic resources to acquire and in what format. What was once an isolated database (for instance, a DIALOG file) can now be found or accessed in a multitude of locations or formats from a variety of vendors. An additional wrinkle is how to balance new electronic acquisitions with traditional print formats or even slightly older electronic resources such as CD-ROMs (with which users are more familiar).

Justifying library purchase decisions has also become increasingly important. When books are purchased, they often appear on new book shelves for browsing by library customers and will then be available in the stacks for use. Electronic resources, in contrast, lack the physical presence of books and journals. When library users and budget authorities ask to see what has been purchased with library funds, CD-ROMs or floppy disks may be shown, but how can one show what has been purchased from an online vendor or an Internet Web site? These issues can be addressed with the careful development of an electronic information resources collection development policy. Realities of the digital collection must include consideration of economic constraints, finding personnel with the proper training, new developments in scholarly publishing, and ever-changing technology.

Librarians are uniquely prepared to tackle this issue because they have previously grappled with the view that digital manifestations of information resources will replace, rather than complement, their physical counterparts. This so-called "paperless society" argument is not new and has been joined, in recent times, by the "library without walls" concept that suggests a time when information will no longer be stored within the pages of books or journals. But this view is extremely polarized and ignores the historical fact that we, as a civilization, have never relied on a single method to access information or on a single format as an information resource. A digital online version of a piece of information simply provides an alternative form of access to that information and the new media classroom is, in the same way, simply an alternative forum for the exchange of ideas. The online environment is not the only interface with students, just the newest.

Information" is a national resource and the lifeblood of national development. It is as crucial for organizations, corporations and nations to gain competitive advantage as it is important to get access to current, up-to-the-minute information to survive in the global market. Therefore, production, acquisition, organization, retrieval and use of information should be seen as a national issue.

Information processing should operate for human prosperity, and should provide achievement of the maximum benefit for everyone and avoid creating information-rich and information-poor in society. The system must relieve the user of as much work as technologies we adopt or use should help us to further those values and certainly shouldn't work against us for example, endangering intellectual freedom. Although information processing systems are capable of self-organization in a large measure, thanks to a certain level of artificial intelligence, to ensure maximum benefit for everyone their evolution should be controlled and inter- co-ordinated on various levels To create the necessary control gear on a state scale, most of the countries have started to develop national information policies. Our strengths include an emphasis on lifelong literacy and education; a focus on selection and quality of information and helping users find the best of what they seek; organization for access; and special concern for young people and the development of their critical information skills. While computer skills may be a new area of training, bibliographic instruction is alive and well but with a different name and a different focus. Information literacy is the byword, whether that means instruction in finding citations in print indexes or using an online database, searching the web, or sending an e-mail to get information.

The book which consists of thirteen research papers contributed to various journals during the course of last decade, looks into all these changes, challenges, issues, strategies and situations of contemporary interest both from users' and providers perspectives. An effort has been made to establish a continuity and linkage among the chapters so as to maintain coherence and consistency in the text. It is hoped that the chapters will sustain readers interest despite some overlapping and repetitions which are bound to creep in such publications.

# 1

# Management of Library Services: Challenge of New Technology

## 1. Introduction

Driven by computers, satellites, laser beams and optical fibres, the information juggernaut has triumphantly entered the 21st century. Whereas the industrial revolution took nearly two centuries to run its course, the Information Revolution has done the job in just three decades. This has given rise, to a new mythology of the information society, where "information technology" *per se* is being presented as the new saviour of the mandkind, opening new vistas for the liberation of human spirit from the bondage of dull routine and the drudgery of mass production. Alvin Toffler argues that new information technologies would lead to an all round "de-massification" of production process, organizational structures, culture and leisure. Individual computer terminals, networked to office consoles or massive databases would enable people to work from their homes, and choose their own working hours (Toffler, 1990).

Many organizations are now heading down the information systems path. Some have made heavy investments in knowledge-sharing networks such as lotus notes, and others have harnessed the power of the World Wide Web. Computer networks with voice and video permit any number of participants across any number of countries. Andersen World Wide, a US based consulting firm, has recently linked its 82,000 people in 360 offices across 76 countries on a system known as "Anet." Data, voice, and video links are all available, and Anderson's professionals are able to form instant groups of expertise around any particular client problem (Hope, 1997).

The world of library and information science could not remain immune to the technological developments, and is witnessing a sea change. The stage has come when the traditional type of library is fast becoming obsolete and meaningless, incapable of coping with the mass of knowledge. Magnetic and optical storage of information, Compact Disc-Read Only Memory (CD-ROM) technology, computerized database and on-line information retrieval have brought all the art treasures of the world at the door-steps of libraries. Electronic mail and voice mail have tied libraries close together even as they disperse geographically. Global networks can move data at speeds of 1.8 kilobytes per second, 50,000 pages of manuscript with each tick of clock. Data transmission speeds, now in development, will move the entire contents of the Library of Congress in just four minutes. Neural networks, the technological surprise going to jump out of the information jack-in-box, will mimic human thought patterns, giving machines the ability, for example, to "mine" data, making independent decisions as they burrow through layers of vast data bases (Harvard, 1993).

## 2. The Genesis of Information Technology

The "growth" and "development" of information technology has been preceded by information explosion. The end of World War II witnessed exponential growth in the publishing rates. The urgent need to cope with "information explosion" and to employ suitable means to handle information work was a major force in the introduction and application of computer and communication technologies so as to meet the user's specific information needs from varied information sources pin-pointedly, expeditiously and exhaustively. Information-handling techniques and their working methods, manual or semi-manual, means and ways used in the past for recording, processing, retrieving and disseminating information were no longer adequate to meet the quantum of information to be handled and hence needed to be replaced by or complemented by computer based systems. The need for automation or application of information technology became all the more urgent in the face of serious resource crunch and escalating cost of publications:

> The escalating cost of goods and services, the steady and stored against the deepening budget and space problems, the demand for service from a growing user population and the availability of new types of materials which can not be treated by conventional methods led to the breakdown of the established operations and created a necessity to look for new approaches to management and organizational set-up (Dubey, 1988).

New Information Technology has provided a way out.

## 3. Information Technology: Components and Applications

The armada of information technologies driving new structures and other changes is formidable. It has three key components:

1. New ways to store information compactly and cheaply, photographic micro forms of various kinds, magnetic storages on tapes and discs, optical storage and video discs.
2. New mechanism to manipulate, scan and store records.
3. New facilities for cheap and rapid transmission of information over long distance-telecomunication systems and networks.

## 4. Developments in Storage Media

Revolution in storage media has been led by computers. The introduction of data processing equipments and procedures into library operation began around 1935 in the United States. The University of Texas Library introduced a circulation system using punched cards. Highly advanced circulation system was installed at Montclair Public Library, New Jersey in 1941. Most of the attempts to utilize computers that originated in libraries were concerned with implementing an acquisition system or a circulation system for lending books or the creation of catalogue cards. A study by a panel of experts under the auspices of Library of Congress reported in 1964 the feasibility of automation of its bibliographic processes and envisaged access to the contents through computer consoles. The Machine Readable Cataloguing (MARC) project that followed established a standard format for exchange of bibliographic information in machine readable form. Interest in mechanized information retrieval has led to research in new indexing techniques. New classification systems, the sequence constructions, statistical analysis of language to create abstracts automatically and improvement in concordances are examples of the variety of subjects studied. The most widely used techniques for indexing by computer, is the Key word-in Context Index (KWIC). Advances in information processing technology have brought attempts to automate the process of classification. A number of mathematical techniques and "Expert System" are being used for analysis of a document contents into a number of subjects. Within the past five years, increasing emphasis has been placed on machine analysis of the syntax and semantics of natural language.

The establishment of various large databases, which are mounted on large computers by on-line host has had a significant impact on the effectiveness and efficiency of the retrieval of information. At library catalogues and indexes are becoming automatically searchable, networks offering access to mechanically readable collections nationwide are coming into being. Automatic information retrieval services have placed the resources of central data banks at the disposal of any one with a personal computer, giving, thus, a tremendous boost to resource sharing. In 1974, the libraries of Yale, Columbia and the Harvard Universities and the New York public library formed the Research Libraries Group (RLG) and went for a common technical system in 1978 naming it Research Library Information Network (RLIN). By 1983, RLG had 15 member institutions and 12 million records in its database. The Washington Library Network (WLN) in 1983, served 95 libraries on the Pacific Northwest. The University of Toronto Library Automation System (UTLAS), a Canadian based on-line bibliographic vendor, in 1983 had contracts with 1800 libraries for products and services and had some 6.5 million records in its database.

On-line searching of external database and feeding of external intelligence into the organization has become a significant and integral part of any information system. Public and academic libraries more interested in the use of such databases for answering queries for information have been vitally affected in their way of handling the queries and supply of current awareness services. In-house databases, incorporating bibliographic references and other information, offering a range of searching facilities from a variety of combination of search terms and logic are coming up rapidly. Some of the large turn-key system suppliers have begun to offer modules which support the maintenance and searching of database of community information.

Computerization of various library house-keeping systems has led to offering of additional services and functions. Statistics regarding various operations, for example, are often a by-product of a computerized system. Within an organization it is having a significant impact on communication and co-operation between branches, sites and departments eliminating duplication in record-creation filing and storage and make it easier to establish and monitor responsibility for specific record management.

### 4.1 *Microform*

A microform may be defined as a document in reduced format. Originally, it was used in libraries to reproduce unique or rare items. More recently, original publications have begun to appear in microform. There are essentially three types of microforms.

### 4.2 *Microfilm*

It is a contact photographic format of a master negative. A brief catalogue entry appears at the top of the card in normal size. From 60 to 80 pages of an average sized book are reproduced on the lower portion of card.

### 4.3 *Microfiche*

It is similar to the micro card in format except that it is on a transparent base created as a positive contact print from a master negative.

### 4.4 *Microprint Card*

It is produced by phototype photolithoraphy, using a high-class paper and special drying inks.

Most commercial publications in microform consist of massive collection of material representing a subject, a period of time, or a geographic area rather than single bibliographic items. A set of Collier's Encyclopaedia can be reduced to a small fraction of its present size and its information stored in computer memory. Such bulky publications as Census of India are now available on microfiche.

Microform is a suitable medium to lessen the problems occurring due to documentation inflation. It helps to store in a very compact form and enables faster retrieval on a low cost. Publications such as indexing and abstracting journals are being rapidly replaced by this media. About 30 per cent of the total scientific journals are available in microforms. The advent of digitizers has facilitated their transmission over distances.

The use of microforms has provided a new job for working librarians in the analysis, planning, implementation and maintenance of the system. Enormous amount of information put in condensed and handy form e.g. microfiches, etc can be transported economically and speedily from one place to any other of the world with the use of communication networks. Since this medium helps dissemination of information to the user's desk, the users have begun to prefer the information to be accessible to them at their work places.

**4.5 *Optical Laser Discs***

Although magnetic media have proved faithful and reliable, there has always been a search for media with higher storage capacities. One of the major new media to enter the market place is the optical or laser disc, which offers high storage capacities. Optical or laser discs are discs that are coated with a material in which laser can create marks. These marks then reflect laser light information encoded as marks and is read by directing a laser on the surface and detecting the reflected light. There are a number of different kinds of optical or laser discs such as read only, write only, or erasable and analogue or digital. The read only digital disc, in the form of CD-ROM is useful for storing video images and can hold digital data by converting it to analogue data. CD-ROM provides a new medium for the mass production and distribution of information. Its peculiar feature lies in the extraordinary storage capacity. A single compact disc of the 120 mm can store over 500 megabytes comparable to the storage capability of 1500 floppy discs or the equivalent of 2,00,000 pages of text. The information stored in sealed environment that is very durable and relatively insensitive to dust or scratches is retrieved through micro computers connected to CD-ROM drive through a controller interface board.

CD-ROM allows access to information under local in-house control and independent of on-line and telecommunication services. A CD-ROM disc can scan easily, marked to any location and can be used repeatedly allowing unlimited access to information without increasing cost. The stored information can, if the user wishes, be accessed interactively, in a friendly and human manner, steering his way to the desired information using an exciting and entertaining procedure. The removal of high cost of purchasing, privacy of searching, accessibility in remote locations, where telecommunication nodes are not available, optical discs can be seen as a medium that will encourage searching by the end user.

### 5. Development in Communication Media

No discussion of technology pertinent to the field of information storage and retrieval would be complete without considering the role of communication. Retrieval at a distance of digital and graphic information pre-supposes the availability of inter-connected communication network. Data communication systems, linked to computers, have made it possible to process information and transmit data to any location instantaneously. In addition the convergence of computers and telecommunication has improved the technology of both contributing areas, and offered new means of communications and data storage such as Electronic Mail, Electronic journal and Videotex document delivery; on-line search and networking are mainly possible due to these new facilities for rapid and cheap transmission of information.

### 6. Document Delivery Services

The ready access to the millions of surrogate references in the online bibliographic databases has led to the increased demand for access to the document themselves.

Lockheed's DIALOG has initiated DIALOG ORDER, a document delivery system which permits the customers of DIALOG index and abstract database to use their terminals to order the full text of documents. A delivery service embracing books, serial and photocopies has been developed by OCLC.

### 6.1 *Videotex*

Videotex system transmits text or graphics stored in computer database via the telephone network for display on television screen connected via electronic interface with full interactive facility. Over 120 public libraries in Britain provide prestel terminal for public user as a means of providing community information. Videotex based community information has forced librarians to re-evaluate and re-design the database and files that they maintain of community information. Libraries can make their catalogue and other databases available through a videotex interface.

### 6.2 *Teletext*

Teletext is a non-interactive form of Videotex and is designed for the general public and mass communication. It is broadcast, received and displayed by a teletext set, which is an adapted television receiver. The data is stored as frames and a pad on television set allows the user to select a specific frame. The best known services in UK are BBC's CEEFAX and independent TV's ORACLE, both of which transmit information of wide public interest. The medium of Teletext is suited to real time information transmission. Public application areas include financial services and electronic publication.

### 6.3 *Fascimile Transmission*

Fax is a means of transmitting a copy of a page of text or graphics to a remote location via telecommunication links. It has been boosted by the adoption of methods of data compression made possible by compact, reliable and inexpensive electronics. Fax is one possible technology for electronics document delivery. For example, the British Library Document Supply Centre is using fax for document delivery. Thus the use of telecommunications is conjunction with computers have made it possible to process information and to transmit it to any location instantaneously.

### 6.4 *Information Technology: Impact on Library Services*

The technological revolution is far from over. We are firmly locked into a cycle of technologies driving further technology. The introduction and application of these modern means have elevated the modern day library to a very high pedestal, improving and altering its image functions and services to a revolutionary extent. Modern librarianship rejects collecting information as an end in itself. The focus now is on dissemination. The reliance on local holdings for meeting user's information needs has given way to extensive use of outside services. Devices for "home information delivery" are becoming operative. The technological transformation facilitates the provision of innovative library service to the patrons outside the physical plant of a library.

The online networking system makes reality of the long aspired resources sharing schemes, cooperative acquisition schemes, co-operative cataloguing and what not. The status report prepared by National Information System for Science and Technology (NISSAT) on bibliographical information processing in India, indicates that there are about 21 organizations in India itself offering computerized bibliographical information service. New information technology has opened up new opportunities, possibilities and area of choice for organizational rearrangements.

The computerized acquisition system has eased the burden for pre-order checking by providing automatic generation of orders, checking of duplicate purchase orders and follow-up action can also be taken automatically. It has speeded up the acquisition, processing work by eliminating a large amount of repetitive and time consuming work. The added entries and the confusion and the controversy inherent in this work has been successfully overcome. Machine readable catalogue is easy to manipulate as it can be searched online and from which a variety of outputs are possible.

The most profound impact of the application of information technology has been in the area of reference service. The number of librarians who flee to stacks in the face of a reference query is diminishing with the arrival of computer terminals. Online retrieval of national and international databanks has placed the entire universe of knowledge at the disposal of libraries and access to technological and scientific data through ability to interact with the computer terminal at constantly decreasing cost, has made a distinct mark on the research and development activities of researchers by consolidating and synthesizing the scientific information on a very large scale.

New information technology has revolutionized the reference service. Development of computer based SDI (Selected Dissemination of Information) which search reference databases such as, chemical abstracts, taps and matches "profiles" with stored references to journal articles and provides the users required references in no time. A number of library subject oriented printed indexes and abstracts are being replaced or supplemented by online access to machine readable version of the same publications. Simply by dialling a telephone number, a terminal in a library is connected with one of the several telecommunication networks to the service agency's computer. Through a simple identification, a searcher specifies which database on the computer is to be searched and then proceeds through interactive dialogue to retrieve pertinent citation.

Online full-text databases containing not just citations to documents but the entire text of documents themselves are available to the users on their workstation. The practical advantages that online indexing and abstracting databases have over their printed counterpart are currency of information and flexibility of searching. Subject orientation, covering material pertinent to a particular decision, in some cases narrowly defined, has been primary focus of the computerized bibliographic storage and retrieval system.

Competitive acquisitions, based on the assumption, the bigger is better, are being replaced by co-operative acquisitions. Libraries are choosing to borrow rather than purchase. Online bibliographic databases are having a significant effect on collection development policy. The longstanding tradition of the inter-library loan is being vastly expanded through the use of computer-produced union catalogues, online catalogue, data communication, facsimile transmission and computer message switching. Compiling a machine readable standard format has greatly facilitated the identification and exact location of a document. Telefacsimile transmission is on its way to become something of a technological dinosaur in this respect, resulting in deduction of expenses of each participating institution and at the same time providing better overall services to all library clientele.

Another response to development in the delivery of information is the emergence of corporate information manager. As information choice becomes more complex and consequences of choice are obvious, organizations with large information related budget are developing information management roles. Librarians are in a favourable position to compete for such a role as well.

Yet another impact of information technology is the trend towards expansion of fee-based services. With increased cost, greater automation and associated capital incentives, new sources of revenue are necessary to sustain more costly but for more effective services that users are becoming accustomed to having. This is leading to extensive commercialization of library services.

Technological development poses two additional challenges to the professional information community. One is the development of a comprehensive standardization programme for library and related information processing system and operations. The other is the development of updated and forward looking curricular materials and methods for information pofessional and potential users.

## 7. Limitations

While computers or terminals can be found in most large libraries or many small ones, traditional library operations have not been substantially altered. The speed, manner and success with which libraries will utilize new systems are uncertain. These will depend on solutions to operational and philosophical problems. Some of the factors responsible for lopsided applications of new information technology can be summed up as follows:

### 7.1 *Attitudes*

Librarian's attitude about automation, user, planning and change are critical elements affecting the use of existing technologies. For many years librarians reacted negatively to any system which altered the existing order of library. Librarians' attitude about new technolog-use are due for re-examination and re-formulation for the successful application of technologies.

### 7.2 *Economics*

The financial constraints which prevent librarians from thinking about new emerging demands of the users are real, particularly for the third world countries.

### 7.3 *User Charges*

The introduction of modern technology, online bibliographic information retrieval systems, databases and their associated out-of-pocket cost has raised the issue of user fee. It needs to be resolved amicably for the proper use and implementation of new technology.

### 7.4 *Lack of Trained Staff*

In countries like India there is a distinct lack of trained staff to handle the new systems. It definitely hampers the utilization of modern means to a great extent.

## 8. Conclusion

The technological revolution has altered the library ecology. It has alerted the user to more than what the individual library holds, creating opportunities and mechanism for rescue operations. Librarians are emerging from the catalogue closet stopping the revolution about the record keeping axis and taking charge of the information revolution. The development of regional, national and international networks is affecting the planning, policy and library functions. Substitutions of non-print forms for distribution for paper dominated systems, and shift from near total reliance on local holding for answering user's needs to extensive use of outside services for accessing larger, remote sources of information are the two most visible side effects. These in turn are leading to substantial changes in the structure of libraries, revenue bases for operations and competencies required of library professionals and users.

Electronic means of transmissions, coupled with magnetic and storage of larger files has enabled in lowering the unit cost, managing ever increasing volumes of information and increasing its effective use. The image of future involves a number of databases available on different computer system and accessible through a variety of different users. The librarians of future will be able to sit at a workstation and call up library catalogue, bibliography databases and other internal system. They will be able to create document via word processing and communicate with other libraries through electronic mail. Teleconferencing and videophones will remove the need for expensive travels. Although many of the components of the scenario are possible already, there remains much work to be done before all system can be effectively interconnected and integrated.

**References**

Dubey, Yogendra P. (1988). "Computer and Telecommunication Technology: A State of Art," in Sharma, C. D. and D. C. Ojha (eds.) *Advances in Library and Information Science*. Jaipur: RBSA Publishers.

Harvard Business School (1992). *Revolution in Real Time: Managing Information Technology in the 1990s*. Boston: Harvard Business School Publishing Division.

Hope, Jeremy and Tony Hope (1997). *Competing in the Third Wave: The Tenkey Management Issues of the Information Age*. Boston: Harvard Business School Publishing Division.

Rowley, Jennifer (1988). *The Basics of Information Technology*. London: Clive Bingley.

Toffler, Alvin (1990). *Power Shift—Knowledge, Wealth and Violence at the Edge of 21st Century*, New York: Bantom Books.

# 2

# Librarianship under Digital Paradigm

## 1. Introduction

The onslaught of computer driven technologies is having a profound effect on library services rendered traditionaly.

As information is becoming a more central topic in society, the profession of librarianship is in a decline.

The paradigm built around the icon of book is fast being replaced by the digital icon.

## 2. The Paradigm Change

Throughout history, librarians have carried out three basic functions. First, they have gathered and protected data; second, they have organised and stored that data according to some system and third, they have distributed that data to users. Each of these functions deserves to be addressed, both as the function has been performed until now and as digital information might change it.

## 3. Librarianship under the Book Paradigm

### 3.1 *Data Collection*

Gathering and protecting data was the greatest challenge to librarians until the modern era. The word data may sound prejudicially modern, but it is meant to encompass books, papers, manuscripts – really any artifact. The physical act of gathering these items was once an inordinate challenge. Books and manuscripts were relatively rare and precious. Such items represented power and wealth and might be perceived as a threat by those who did not have or use them. Books and manuscripts allowed for the growth and spread of ideas, representing an almost magical power in a largely illiterate world.

But the challenge of just getting information is now largely gone. Modern industrial printing has changed this. Books appear in great number and volumes. The function of gathering has been transformed into the challenge of choosing. The problem is no longer finding information, but sorting and filtering it.

Today's librarian is actually someone who is filtering a flood of information, most likely with no real ability to control or preserve what they already have. The modern librarian may still be called upon to show courage to retain certain titles in the face of political pressure, but they will face the problem of finding the necessary resources to purchase all the information desired, not the problem of finding the information itself.

### 3.2 *Organising Data*

The modern profession of librarianship has emphasised developing methods for organising information. As the problem of gathering waned, the problem of organising grew. The challenge was met in two ways.

The first is the most basic – how should one organise the data? The data here was largely books. As physical objects, books needed to be put somewhere. What methods should be used to shelve them? Of course one could simply shelve them in the order in which they arrived. This system, constructed around a need to record each arrival, might serve in certain situations.

This need led to the development of the pre-coordinated index, an index designed before having access to the information. It is the opposite, for example, of indexing a book, where the information is already there for the indexer to describe. A pre-coordinated index provides a systematic description of every possible topic into which books will be regrouped.

The challenge of creating a system that provides a topical universe covering every possibility is not trivial. Melvyl Dewey supplied his Dewey Decimal System, a broadly based but comprehensive system that worked well enough with fairly general collections, and one still used in some smaller collections. But the size of many libraries outstripped the organisational specificity of the Dewey system. As the great libraries grew, more precision was needed. Smaller specialised libraries grew, more precision was needed. Smaller specialised libraries too needed more depth of description for the collection they housed. It was useless to a library to have all its books carry the same classification designation. Some libraries opted to create their own classification systems, each of which represented the intellectual effort of a librarian grappling with information.

As many books cover more than one topic, but the book could only be put in one place, the library user needed a way to find a book without having to puzzle out the classification system. It was to meet this need that the other great intellectual effort of descriptive cataloguing and subject analysis was undertaken.

Subject and descriptive cataloguing is the process of precisely describing each book and creating a separate set of records reflecting those descriptions. These records describe the books according to a standard protocol, thus enabling the library user to find a specific book by any one of a number of access routes.

### 3.3 *Distributing Information*

The third function of librarians has been increasingly emphasised in recent years. At the most basic level, distributing information in the form of books is simply a matter of allowing physical access to them.

Librarians created two solutions for this problem. One was an increased level of reference assistance. This concept included more aggressive forms of outreach to the library patrons and the development of pathfinders, handouts, library guides and other reference tools. Reference librarians debated the ethics of how much to involve themselves in the library patrons reference questions. The dynamics of the reference interview and the best strategies for helping the user find what they needed were explored in professional literature and in the library schools as librarianship became increasingly concerned with issues of communication.

A second solution to the problem was called bibliographic institution. Librarians were cast as teachers whose mission was to guide the users by teaching them research skills. This form of instruction placed the librarian in a proactive position. Rather than serving only as a guardian and organiser of information, the librarian became one to assist in its interpretation and use. This is not to say that a librarian had not previously played a role as adviser and helper, but the role of teacher grew in importance.

## 4. Librarianship Under Digital Paradigm

The paradigm for the use of information has changed. In the light of this change, what will happen to the traditional functions of librarians? Will they be preserved, reformed, or destroyed?

### 4.1 *Gathering Data*

The old model of the library was based on a conception

deeply rooted in the idea of the book. Indeed librarians, the profession that served the information needs of society, named itself after the building that housed the books. Librarians went forth into the world to gather information and bring it back to the library where they guarded it. If it was a rare item, because it was scarce or had a special quality of binding or illustration, it was placed in special storage. But every item that was brought back to the library was owned in a physical sense by the library. It might be borrowed by a user, but when it was taken, careful records were maintained of who had it and where. Each physical entity, no matter how banal its information, was physically unique. Once again, many of the common stereotypes of librarians grew out of this monitoring function. The library card was one's ticket to privilege, allowing a person to use the books by physically removing them. The systems for monitoring the book's use, especially the system of enforcement like library fine, became a fixture in comedic literature. Librarians were seen as the book police.[1]

Some materials were so costly, so large, or so likely to be needed by large numbers of people that they could never be allowed to leave the library building. These items were not necessarily rare, but they were valuable and thus had to be controlled. Once again, it is the physical nature of the book that makes this action necessary. The book can only exist in one place at a time, and only one user at a time can comfortably use a single volume.

The new paradigm of digital information completely changes this set of relationships. Digital information does not exist in one tangible place. It cannot be stored in an edifice, nor can it be owned and controlled like a book. It lacks all of the attributes of physicality. The data is stored in electronic form and may be scattered throughout the memory of the storage vehicle. When one wishes to use it one can take a copy away while leaving the original in place. Use by one patron in no way precludes use by others.

Nor does the information have to be returned – it can be retained by the user. There is no need for guarding it and monitoring the use, at least no need related to the librarians function. The digital information beginning to flood the information marketplaces is infinitely elastic and uncontrollable. The entire concept of ownership will have to be rethought. But regardless of the shape that the new conceptualisation takes, it will not replicate the library model.[2]

If individuals who need information can gain access to it via a home computer and a modem, they will not have to come to the library at all. While some information may continue to be restricted due to its content, or have its access limited by being priced on a pre-use basis, there will be no rationale for screening users from information since the information no longer possesses physical attributes.

For librarianship this will be most unsettling. No longer will libraries be curators or caretakers of information. There will be no need. Librarians will have to choose what data to purchase or lease and how to structure its availability, but most of the rest of the basic tenets of the old paradigm are gone. At the Research Libraries Group Symposium on electronic libraries held in Menlo Park in August 1993, Douglas Van Howeeling of the University of Michigan stated that librarians must realise that in the information age, they are retailers of information, discount retailers, in fact. In the old world of information warehouses, librarians guarded the information and protected it from a sometimes hostile world. In the new world, librarians will be facilitating patrons' use of information moving information out, packaging it, marketing it.[3]

### 4.2 *Organising Information*

It was the tangible nature of the book, its property of occupying one particular space, that led to all the efforts to describe it and categorise it. Once the book was assigned to a location, no matter how well thoughtout that location, system had to be designed to lead users to the book from various starting points. It was never apparent that the physical nature of the book dictated these decisions until digital information demonstrated that the tangible form of the book was inherently limiting.

Digital information does not occupy a physical space in the same sense that a book does. The electrons that make up a body of digital information do not sit on a shelf, they may be scattered throughout the storage mechanism used and only reconfigured as needed. In a full-text digital on-line system, the finding tool does not lead one to the single specific location of a physical manifestation of information, instead the tools recreate the information. In other words, one formulates the parameters of the search for information and is then given appropriates results. It a real sense, full-text on-line systems create a customised result for use for the results of the search to go somewhere else. Now instead of the user going brought directly to them, almost instantaneously.

Since the information is not limited to one location, and since it does not have to be found in the old sense, it does not have to be classified. But proper paths for finding information have to be embedded within it to allow for its retrieval for later use. But this function of creating pathways or retrieval is usually the work of database creator, not the librarian. Just as librarians do not prepare the index or table of contents in books, they do not prepare the search engines for most databases. All of the indexes can become one enormous index, made manageable by the search engines replacing the old organisational systems. Once again the mediating function of the information gatherer as librarian is rendered unnecessary by the nature of digital information and by electronic publishers' development of their own user-friendly search systems.[4]

These search engines, which allow the user to search databases by hooks embedded in the data, or by Boolean search connectors, and to penetrate the full text of documents, are rendering my form of catalogue less and less useful for most users.

Librarians have long known that most people had trouble using card catalogues. Most library users are just not good subject searchers. Being precise and complete in describing each book calls for a level of detail and a complexity of organisation that rendered the systems of information location produced counter productive for everyone but the expert.

Now the point is moot. If one can search for information through a modern on-line bibliographic system using a word in title search that does not require precision or the use of protocols, one seldom will resort to any subject that, by its nature, requires protocols and hierarchical judgments.

As such systems develop, they will be applied to the information that exists in digital form. Thus, as more and more information is converted to that form, these systems will replace any intermediary engine developed by librarians. One could debate at length the speed with which existing information will be put in digital form via imaging or some related technology, but one must assume that where there is a market for such conversion, it will occur. As it does, the role of librarians and the systems of organising and classifying information that they have so carefully developed will grow less and less relevant.

### 4.3 *Distribution of Information*

The most puzzling part of the paradigm shift is its impact on the distribution of information by librarians. Digital information raises a host of distribution related questions that are moving to the centre of the stage of societal debate. The potential of the Internet and information superhighway are everywhere among us, indeed, to the radicals, the game of distributing information, is lost to librarianship already. For them the mergers of telephones companies and cable television operations have more to say about the use of information than anything associated with the concept of shelving books.

Business schools are training management information systems specialists, computer science departments are training database managers and undergraduate programmes are beginning to offer majors in information. These people see information as a commodity. The new corporate heroes are figures like Bill Gates at Microsoft, the symbol of information manipulation and the new paradigm.[5]

This puts librarianship's old model for the distribution of information in jeopardy. The radicals within the profession do not want to be called librarians, they went to cut loose the old heritage and move on. They contend that, in any case, the life and energy of information is not found in the halls of any library school. Those halls are filled with librarians; the wrong horses are in place. There may continue to be library schools, but they will train information workers who will be clerical and who will never hope to aspire to the humanitarian goal of public enlightenment.

## 5. Conclusion

Yet it remains crucial to remember the role of the user. Expert users of the new information, the techno-cowboys of the new generation, will need little help. But the vast majority of users in any library will be average and they will need to be taught how to navigate the increasingly digitised library. Some believed that as digital systems proliferated, typical users would grow more and more sophisticated until they no longer needed librarians. This theory is demonstrably wrong. As the systems have developed, users have grown used to icon-based, menu-driven systems that are extremely easy to use. The average user today expects to be prompted by systems that call for no training and operate intuitively. Large scale database systems have yet to meet these expectations, so, in fact, users need more help than ever. The librarian's role can be to provide that help.

Librarians must recognise that the modern distribution function consists of holding the digital hand of a database user, serving as the neutral expert who can credibly advise users on what the using is. To do this, librarians must insert themselves in the process of creating, organising and introducing these databases. This is new and intimidating but it is the profession's last hope.

It will help to remember that someone will have to fill the helping function. Librarians would be the best choice since the profession is already in place, but it will have to show that it is ready and it will have to move quickly. In four or five years, the executives of the large database companies will not be coming to library meetings asking for help. They either will have received help from librarians or they will have gone elsewhere, but whatever the source, the goal will have sailed. Librarianship should do everything that it can to be on that boat.

## References


1. Raymond Kurzweil, "*The Future of Libraries, Part 2: The End of Books*." Library Journal, 15 February 1992.
2. Coraghessan Boyle, *Descent of Man Stories* (Boston, 1979).
3. Umberto Eco, *The Name of the Rose*, trans. William Weaver (San Diego, 1983).
4. Robert C Berring, "Full-text Databases and Legal Research Backing into the Future," *High Technology Law Journal 1* (Spring 1986), especially note 31.
5. Jay McInerney, "*The Way of All Text*," The New Yorker, September 20, 1993, 128.

# 3

# New Information Environment: A Literature Review

## 1. Introduction

As electronic Information is spreading its wings the library literature is being exceedingly replete with phrases such as "information age", "global information economy", "virtual library", "information superhighway." The stage has come when traditional type of library is fast becoming obsolete and meaningless, incapable of coping with the mass of knowledge. The very frequency of terms, as applied to computer-based technology and communication systems, and to organization strategies and structure, may have dulled our alertness to the magnitude of the fundamental changes that are emerging while also clouding our ability to see clearly what is indeed changing and what remains essentially the same.

## 2. Changes

However despite all these revolutionary changes, the values that are the foundation of the library profession should remain the same in the new century. These values of service, quality, universal access, and cooperation are not threatened unless librarians ignore them. The way in which these values are translated into operations and activities, though, will undergo substantial change.

There is, of course, no "age" that has not depended on information as a basic element in all components of society, including the underpinnings of the economy. What is the difference, then, in today's world that such hyperbole as "information age", and the like is applied to information and, more specifically to information technology?

Furthermore, information technology has created a sense of urgency and has created new possibilities for the development of new products and delivery of services. At the same time, the impact of information technology in communication processes and connections has challenged the basic assumptions about organization structure, working relationships and the nature and quality of service.

Some of the characteristics of the current and emerging information environment in which librarians will have to function include:

- greater access to a range of information,
- increased speed in acquiring information,
- greater complexity in locating, analyzing, and linking information,
- constantly changing technology,
- lack of standardization of both hardware and software,
- continuous learning for users and library staff,
- substantial financial investment for technology.

The reality, then, is that whatever labels — information age, global information village — are used to describe the current environment, librarians need to find ways to respond effectively and innovatively to a very different landscape in meeting user expectations. This is needed if librarians and libraries are to flourish, or even survive, within their institutions.

Librarians need to see themselves and their libraries as providing bridges to the past and gateways to the future.

They need to establish partnerships, coalitions, and connections — technological, personal and organizational — to ensure a central role in the twenty-first century.

Universities assemble people to work together in the creation of new knowledge and the transmission of previously developed knowledge, the challenge for librarians is to rethink and recreate their place in this process, and to move the focus away from the library as a physical space to a new reality of the library providing knowledgeable people who offer a variety of essential and timely services.[1]

Librarians are challenged to explore new opportunities and implement changes in the following critical areas:

- establish new roles and responsibilities for library professionals that result in quality services,
- determine knowledge, skills and abilities required for all staff, create new partnerships,
- redesign organization & realign the culture.

### 3. Implications of Change

The librarian's role should be characterized by visibility and vitality. Specifically, librarians should be highly visible and well integrated into the activities of their institution and the community they serve. This means that librarians should be valued as essential to the teaching, learning and research activities. Librarians, not solely the collections or the library building, should be valued and considered as an integral member parts of the teaching and research team.

Most important, librarians should be seen as part of the solution — contributing to quality education, rather than as part of the problem — contributing to escalating costs. Librarians need to be bold and imaginative in defining their role and decisive in acting upon it. They should be visionaries in conceiving the present and imagining the future and they should be willing to take the risks inherent in translating their vision into action.

What activities, services should librarians develop and strengthen in order to transform themselves into an integrated role within the academic enterprise at the beginning of the new century? Further description of the following areas indicates that there is not only a need for reshaping of traditional services but also a requirement for the development of entirely new services in the emerging networked information environment.

- User Education
- Knowledge Management
- Organization of Networked Information Resources
- Information Policy Development
- Electronic Publishing & Curriculum Development
- Strategic and Operational Planning

**4. Education of User Community**

The central and essential role for librarians as teachers cannot be overemphasized. Librarians need to embrace a broad concept for user education, one in which they see themselves as actively contributing to the educational programs of the organization.

The concept of the teaching library and the librarian as a teacher will require a fundamental shift in the role of professionals. The historic role for the library and librarians has largely been collection and building centered with the individual (faculty or student) coming to the library to seek assistance or to locate material. The new paradigm of the teaching library, librarian as a teacher, is one in which librarians actively find users in a variety of settings to provide instruction about information resources and to assist them in acquiring skills in locating, evaluating and using a variety of methods of information, location and presentation such as interactive networks, multimedia, compiler instructed instructions and at different locations, such as labs, workrooms and classrooms librarians will create almost a "library without walls".

Instructional programs, designed to assist all members of the university, from the new student to the experienced faculty or researcher, in learning and remaining current with information resources (in all formats) will be a priority. Content for library instruction will range from general orientation on information resources to instruction in the complexities of using, and even developing sophisticated electronic databases to assisting faculty in incorporating multi-media resources into their courses. The objective within a very robust instructional program will be to integrate the basic concept of "information literacy" with the more complex concept of "informatics" relevant to a particular program, researcher or student.

Additionally, librarians will need to give attention to the information needs of students taking courses away from the campus and the faculty who teach in this environment who need to access books, journals and other resources. Students in a distance education setting will need to receive instruction on information retrieval and evaluation as well as obtain reasonable access to information related to their learning while faculty are likely to need all of the same resources and support of those on campus.

The teaching librarian suggests a broader and more integrated role than the passive nature of reference desk service in which professionals wait for the user to determine if he/she has a question and then to ask it. The teaching librarian goes beyond the idea of tours of the library or providing written handouts or even instruction on bibliographic sources. The teaching librarian embodies an outreach mindset, one in which librarians define a range of information needs of their varied user community (faculty, researchers, undergraduate and graduate students), and design and present instruction in a variety of formats (lecture, self-paced learning, group and individual learning) and at different venues (in a library, in a classroom, dormitory, over the Internet, computer assisted tutorial) to meet these needs.

Library personnel should also assist the faculty to search information relevant to their work using networked resources and through other latest methods of information with which the faculty members are yet not familiar.

Some faculty would want to design and develop their own multimedia products for teaching while others would want to identify and integrate electronic products (both multimedia and networked resources) into their courses. Whether an instructor is integrating existing resources into the curriculum or developing new ones, they must familiarise themselves with new technologies, software and hardware, and learn about new resources and how to use them in relation to the course objectives. In addition, of course, faculty would be exploring and testing approaches different from the lecture model. Librarians can have a central role in assisting faculty with developing skills and facility with the constantly changing technologies and information products.

In order to act on a new concept of user education that is innovative in nature, librarians will have to rethink the structure of traditional reference and bibliographic instruction services. Considerable staff resources would be required to implement such a program and this means that it will not be possible to continue to provide all services that have been offered in the past. Some undesirable operations would have to be relinquished in order to move into these new endeavors.

### 5. Knowledge Management

Another direction for librarians to pursue in shaping their role and services for the future is knowledge management. Richard Lucier[2] states that a knowledge management environment "embraces the entire information-transfer cycle, from the creation, structuring, and representation of information to its dissemination and use." This moves librarians beyond their present role of storage, bibliographic organization, and retrieval into the world of information transfer and creation. The changes occurring in the networked information environment increase the opportunities for librarians to shift and broaden their involvement in the information and scholarly process.

The concept of knowledge management embraces the need to organize large data files, and to link and integrate different but related files and databases to one another so that users can move between and among related resources efficiently. The knowledge management activity requires multidisciplinary teams consisting of faculty-researchers, librarians-information specialists, and technologists-software specialists in order to address the many complex content and technology issues.

As a new enterprise, librarians would have to acquire new skills and abilities and establish priorities in relation to other more traditional activities in order to have the time and energy to move into the knowledge management enterprise. The work is there, waiting to be addressed. Users, particularly researchers, are open to assistance from librarians as is evident from the experience of librarians within the medical community. Librarians, with their knowledge of information organization and access, existing electronic resources, and subject expertise are highly qualified to act as partners in creating new information products and new processes for the management of information databases.

### 6. Online Information Resources

Another activity for which librarians need to accept responsibility and to exercise influence is in the organization of networked information resources. The Internet offers a powerful new way to communicate and gain access to information of all types. In describing the network and software products more generally, Ted Nelson[3] says "what we are seeing out there is a tangled nightmare" and he characterizes the situation as one in which we are increasingly prisoners of clever technologists.

Librarians need to take initiatives for creating better organizations and access to what is available on the Internet. A virtual library is virtually useless if individuals have no structure from which to search and identify the materials they want or to establish the authenticity of materials which are found.

This requires that librarians broaden their view of cataloguing to include electronic resources both those generated and stored on local networks along with sources on the Internet. Beyond, the traditional understanding of cataloguing applied to electronic and networked resources, though librarians have a responsibility and a role to address the issue of authenticity of documents on the network. In the United States, Fred W. Weingarten[4], senior policy advisory at The American Library Association, says that "since electronic information is so easily reproduced and just as easily changed, we will also rediscover a problem from the pre-Gutenberg age of scribes: the search for the original source." So not only will librarians need to be able to provide intellectual and physical access to networked resources, but they would also need to contribute to the process of establishing the authenticity for these sources.

## 7. Information Policy Development

Another activity requiring continuing attention and leadership from librarians is the development of information policies. There is a range of information policy issues for which immediate and ongoing attention is needed. These issues should be addressed by librarians along with faculty, technologists, and university administrators. Certainly the issue around costs for access to electronic information and instructional software and hardware will need to be addressed. If end-users have to pay for all of these costs then there is a good likelihood that information "have" and "have nots" will emerge. This would be a serious problem in higher education where information is central to the entire process of learning and research.

Beyond the individual institution, librarians have a responsibility on a national level to raise policy issues and to take a clear position on these issues. For example, librarians should be vocal on the issues of intellectual property rights and also access to information by citizens. Weingarten has described an activist role for librarians. He states that there are four currents of information — commercial, private, public, and governmental — and that "librarians will have to be involved in managing the boundaries [within cyberspace] between the public space and the commercial and government environments." He goes on to say that "when the need for public information comes into conflict with the needs of commerce . . . librarians argue for a balance that takes into account the principles of public access to information and of free space, . . . they must be strong voices... "

There are number of other policy issues that require open discussion and redefinition in the information technology environment including censorship and privacy. Librarians should assume a key leadership position in their institutions and communities, and on a national level, in identifying policy issues and contributing to the definition of coherent and fair policies in the networked information world.

### 8. Electronic Publishing

Electronic publishing will become commonplace at many places as faculty and researchers who serve on editorial boards seek ways to shift existing journals into this format while others seek to establish new and competitive electronic publications.

There is a definite role for librarians in this endeavor. Librarians can offer their resources — technological and human — to provide a site for developing, testing and archiving electronic publications. This activity requires a collaborative effort among librarians, faculty as the subject specialists, and technologists. A range of materials already being published and/or issued in electronic format by universities includes the "pre-print" distribution of papers by scholars, and the reissuing in electronic format of papers already published in print when copyright clearance is received; papers from university symposia or conferences; referred journals; and multimedia products developed by university staff.

In all of these electronic publishing efforts whether working with faculty or focusing on the electronic distribution of specific library-held resources, librarians can contribute in a number of ways. Specifically, librarians can contribute to the organization of electronic information in order to ensure access, they can contribute to the testing of software applications for a specific project, and to addressing issues surrounding intellectual property. Finally, librarians, as they have in the past, have an important role in the archival function.

Strategic planning should be a fundamental concept that librarians incorporate into their daily activities. In the overall, they need to give greater attention to strategic planning at the organization and departmental level, and then integrate these strategic plans into the goals and activities of individual professionals.

For strategic planning to be worthwhile, the staff throughout the organization need to be involved in the planning process and need to understand the importance of this activity in relation to allocation of scarce resources — staff assignments as well as funds for equipment, space and collections. And there is a need to achieve consensus around the priorities and directions for the organization. Finally a strategic plan provides an important tool to establish accountability both within the library and to external constituencies.

Shaughnessy[5] points out, "accountability extends beyond the domain of budgets, fund accounts, and expenditures. It includes all of an organization's assets . . . [including] time on task." He concludes that librarians need to "focus on those activities and programs that are mission critical."

Strategic planning involves assessment and evaluation, cost-benefit analysis, both short- and long-term projection, and innovation. The strategic planning process should involve not only staff throughout the library, but individuals from the user community as well as other individuals and groups within the institution that will be instrumental in the success of the strategic plan.

In an environment of constant change, librarians will have to challenge traditions and assumptions regarding all aspects of library service. A self-critical and evaluative approach to all operations and functions will be essential along with a willingness to make decision based on facts and user needs instead of on personal feelings or "because we've always done it that way." A reliance on intuitive feelings or past experience is indefensible as a basis for allocating scarce resources, which is what decisions regarding operations and services represent. Equally important will be for library professionals to exercise a far greater degree of risk-taking, the willingness to take action when confronting an unfamiliar or unpredictable situation. In a time of rapid change, it will be necessary for decisions to be reached in a timely manner without the luxury of lengthy deliberations.

With the increasing costs to operate libraries, particularly the enormous investment for technology along with the expenditures for staff and collections in all formats, professionals should be able to think and act strategically and to articulate clearly the strategic directions and priorities to those outside of the library organization.

### 9. Acquiring New Knowledge, Skills, Abilities

If the scope and nature of librarians' role in the networked information environment are to be redefined and expanded, then much attention is needed in several aspects of personal and professional development.

It is essential that library professionals continuously acquire new knowledge and skills to ensure that they remain a vital part of information services of the future. Librarians are learning about a complex range of electronic resources and systems and are addressing complex issues involving information resource selection, cataloging, and copyright while also expanding user education to include new resources and systems. Librarians need to be able to design databases for their own use, assist faculty in such efforts, develop computer-assisted instructional programs for staff and user learning and integrate new technologies into service while assisting users in learning how to apply the same for their work.

Beyond acquiring specific knowledge and skills, it is necessary for library staff to accept different expectations regarding their work, their working relationships and the environment in which they work. They need to develop strategies that allow them to work comfortably and effectively in the turmoil of the academic and information environments.

### 10. Partnerships and Collaboration

All organizations including universities are in a period of transformation and librarians should use this period of change to establish, refocus and strengthen partnerships with other professionals groups within their institutions. There are two significant groups with which library professionals should establish strong collaborative relationships: faculty and technologists.

Historically librarians have always had a strong link to the faculty as teachers and researchers but if professionals are to create a different and more dynamic role for themselves on campus, then the nature of this relationship may need to alter. In order for a real partnership to succeed, librarians need to see themselves as part of the teaching and research endeavor, and participate as an active and integral member of the education team. A fundamental tenet of a partnership or collaboration is one of peers working and communicating together. This requires that those involved — librarians and faculty — be equal within the activities and life of the partnership. And this occurs when there is mutual respect for what each person contributes to the relationship. Peter Drucker[6] in his article The New Society of Organizations, states that the "modern organization . . . has to be an organization of equals, of colleagues and associates. No knowledge ranks higher than another. Each is judged by its contribution to the common task rather than by an inherent superiority or inferiority."

Library professionals also need to reshape and strengthen their relationships with computer specialists and technologists in their institutions. Carol Barone[7] Vice Chancellor Information Technology at UC-Davis, has described the fundamental need to establish robust partnerships. She states, "we need each other! Complex tasks and rapid change require collaborative effort to succeed. Chaotic environments require mutual support. The best and most creative answers to problems are the result of synthesizing many ideas and viewpoints."

If librarians are prepared to absorb and even help shape the magnitude of predicted change into the next century then it will be important for them to realign their relationships within the institution so that strong partnerships exist to provide us with necessary support as well as knowledge for meeting the challenges ahead.

**11. Reengineering the Organisation**

All organizations are in a period of transformation including universities and their libraries with information technology acting as both a catalyst and an instrument of change. Billings[8] views libraries as "organic, living, changing bodies of information, and are becoming increasingly 'bionic' as their traditional, printed resources are being enhanced and extended through electronic technology."

There are many examples in libraries that reflect these principles for organizing work. Work is segmented into functional departments to simplify complex work for the staff, although not necessarily for the user. Libraries have multiple processing departments such as acquisitions, cataloging, binding, marking, and shelving. Direct user services require that the client (faculty, student, staff) come to the library and often to multiple service points to have questions answered, to search and borrow materials, and participate in instructional sessions.

Library professionals should be less concerned with an organization that reflects order and symmetry, comfort, and familiarity than with encouraging action and decision-making, risk, and innovation throughout the organization. Keen[9] states that the mature organization, with its "long-established norms of stability and security must be replaced with new values such as speed, simplicity, and unparalleled customer service, and a self-confident, empowered work force." While a change in library organization structure and culture is necessary, it is important to acknowledge that an organization is not an abstract concept or a piece of paper with boxes and lines but a living organism, a society comprised of people, feelings, attitudes, expectations, and needs. A significant change in the organizational structure may represent a very uncomfortable change for some individuals, particularly as lines blur and responsibilities and authority overlap.

It is essential to recognize that the strength of the library is the staff and that people can be fragile and, therefore, the organization will exhibit this same fragility. As change is undertaken, staff should be involved in some manner in the decisions that create major shifts so that they understand the reasons for changes. In this way, staff are more likely to develop a commitment to required changes in the organization and culture and, by extension, their own behavior.

The organization design for academic libraries in the future will not be built on a single model as has been largely true to date. While there will be great difference among libraries based on individual institutional needs and culture, teamwork should be central to the library organization of the future. Librarians should explore an organization design that relies on teams as the primary way that work is accomplished, decisions reached, and service delivered. Keen suggests that organizations in this intense information environment should shift from "organizing by division of labor to organizing by division of knowledge." The division of knowledge "captures an obvious reality of work in an era of rapid change and uncertainty," and is another way to conceive teamwork.

Library staff who are struggling to keep up with the demands in today's work environment require, indeed deserve, new ways for accomplishing their work. The redesign of the library organization is imperative if we are to move rapidly and with an entrepreneurial spirit in the delivery of services in the current interactive high-speed communication environment.

In order to make the transition from a structure that has been heavily hierarchical and segmented to one that is fluid and flexible, library professionals need to experiment and explore, remain open to considering new approaches, and keep the user as the central focus in any organizational design.

## 12. Conclusion

Although the new developments in information technology are challenging, even overwhelming, the real challenges that we face are not technical in nature. Instead it is the need to imagine and implement change that will translate traditional values into the networked and electronic information in future. In order for librarians to influence and shape the future of information services within the highly technological and global information environment, a change in vision is essential followed by a change in personal knowledge, perspective and behavior. The change required by individuals is the greatest challenge we face in new century!

## References

1. Van Houweling, Douglas E. Knowledge Services in the Digitized World: Possibilities & Strategies. In Electronic Access to Information: A New Services Paradigm . Mountain View, Ca.: The Research Libraries Group, 1994.
2. Lucier, Richard. Knowledge Management: Refining Roles in Scientific Communication. in New Technologies and New Directions. Proceedings from the Symposium on Scholarly Communication . George R. Boynton and Sheila D. Creth. ed. Westport, Ct.: Meckler Publishing, 1993, p. 97.
3. Nelson, Ted. Freedom and Power in New Technologies and New Directions: Proceedings from the Symposium on Scholarly Communication . George R. Boynton and Sheila D. Creth. ed. Westport, Ct.: Meckler Publishing, 1983, p. 2.
4. Weingarten, Fred W. Five Great Roles for Libraries and Librarians within the NII.American Libraries, 1996, p.17.

5. Shaughnessy, Thomas W. The Library Director as Change Agent. Unpublished talk given at University of North Carolina, Chapel Hill, 1992, p. 17.
6. Drucker, Peter. The New Society of Organizations. *Harvard Business Review*. (70) 1992, p. 95.
7. Barone, Carol A. New Interpretations of Old Rules, or If the Ocean Is On the Right You Are Headed North. Cause/Effect 16, 1993, p. 76.
8. Billings, Harold. The Bionic Library: Providing Information in the Digital Age. *The Texas Business Review*, 1996.
9. Keen, Peter G.W. Redesigning the Organization Through Information Technology. *Planning Review* (19), 1991, p. 8.

# 4

# Converging Vision of Library Service for Off-Campus/ Distance Education

## 1. Introduction

The future of library service for off-campus/distance education is discussed from the perspective of a set of commonly held assumptions regarding higher education. One assumption is that distance education is a growth industry for higher education institutions, as well as for commercial providers. Some have predicted that within ten years, 50% of students enrolled in higher education will be distance learners or will be studying in a distance learning environment.[1]

A second assumption is that off-campus students are at a disadvantage compared to their on-campus counterparts, in part, because of the lack of personal contact with faculty and other students and because of problems in gaining access to library staff and resources. A third assumption is that powerful and pervasive interactive technologies will continue to improve the delivery of education and library support at a distance.

## 2. Educational Process

Whether we agree or disagree with these assumptions, we cannot ignore their impact on each of the stakeholders in the educational process: administrators, students, faculty, accrediting bodies, and librarians. For administrators, the problem is clearly one of economics. Libraries are expensive, and resources are not easily duplicated at satellite sites. In the past, administrators have been unable to fund equally and staff off-campus facilities at desired levels.

In the future, technology may help to alleviate the problem as electronic access can be provided to many more resources than libraries are able to purchase with diminishing budgets. For students with job and family constraints, the need for pursuing an education at a distance may mean the difference between having an education or not having one at all, making any disadvantages in terms of academic isolation an acceptable trade-off. In the future, technology can help to reduce the isolation by proiding many options for human interaction through electronic communication. For faculty, it is important that academic standards apply equally to off-campus classes. They need to be able to make library assignments knowing that distance students are able to access the library to complete them. In the future, technology will help to bridge the gap between the distant learner and the library. For accrediting bodies, standards and the review process can bring about the measure of quality assurance needed to bring off-campus programs into the higher education manistream. In the future, technology will enhance delivery of education and access to libraries making it important to re-examine the standards to insure their relevance to an evolving academic setting. For libraries, the potential for user-centred, rather than library-centered, service will be enhanced, as less emphasis is placed on building collections and more on providing access to resources.

### 3. Convergence of Vision

In this context, there will be a convergence of off-campus library service with the library's need to serve a growing number of distance learners. Libraries and librarians will have to build new paradigms to serve the many invisible users remotely accessing library catalogues and online databases. The extended campus will be a part of every library's future for two reasons.

First, as more emphasis is placed on providing access to information, and less on building collections, the philosophy of library service that required users to come to the library for help and resources will no longer be dominant. Along with the paradigm shift to the electronic library will come the need for a new client-centered philosophy that encompasses remote users and distance learners. Service to the extended campus will become more the norm rather than the exception, and the "client-centered service models developed for distant learners will move library service to off-campus and distance education into the forefront."[2]

Second, as technology is used to further library connectivity, we can anticipate significant advances in the delivery of library support to off-campus/distant learners, minimizing the physical disadvantages previously encountered. With more and more academic libraries forming consortia on a state-wise basis to provide common access to electronic records, there will be a kaleidoscope of options for distant learners to choose from in terms of Internet and web access, full-text retrieval, seamless document delivery from publisher to workstation, online reference service, and electronic communication. While geographic isolation and social disadvantage cannot be wholly eliminated for the distant learner, improvements can be anticipated in this area with existing technological advances. In the present multimedia, interactive, electronic environment, access to instruction and resources is greatly facilitated. Socialization of students can be accomplished through the use of e-mail, and electronic mentoring can help to compensate for the lack of faculty and student face-to-face contact. Electronic chat rooms can further enhance communications among distant learners. With the aid of powerful interactive technologies and the forging of statewise and regional alliances, education and library support will produce new synergies for cooperation in the absence of walls and institutions. Home librarians, not just off-campus librarians, will serve remote users and distant learners. This convergence will place both on the same trajectory, and distant learners will benefit from the new synergies developed.

### 4. Optimal Services for Off-Campus Students

The supplying of library services will become highly competitive, and libraries may choose to outsource the provision of services to other institutions. In Australia, for example, the Open Learning Agency has recently contracted with the University of South Australia to provide library services for their 5,000 or so students throughout Australia.[3] In the best tradition of economic rationalism, librarians will need to consider profit margins, performance standards, benchmarking, etc. They also need to acquire a much clearer idea of the true cost of services.

### 5. Meeting the Costs

First, we must see to it that the off-campus service has an adequate budget and staff, which in turn depends on the recognition and acceptance by the administration that they are obligated to support the library needs of off-campus students. Second, we need to target various categories of users and publicize the services which will most benefit their studies. Third, we need to be pro-active in soliciting class reading lists, reserve items, and suggested titles for acquisition from academic staff and faculty. It is of little use to advertise the availability of a library service if the fill rate for requests is, say, only 60%. Furthermore, users should be given a wide variety of convenient and easy methods for requesting services, such as contact by mail, fax, telephone, email, and direct ordering from the catalogue and the World Wide Web. We must be able to offer guaranteed turnaround times for processing requests as stated in performance standards and, ideally, courier delivery of books with a prepaid return envelope provided. Once copyright hurdles have been cleared, we should also be able to supply scanned documents from electronic reserve collection to student desktops. And finally, we need to keep appropriate statistics and cost data so that we know how the budget has been spent.

**6. Use of Information Technology**

There is little doubt that computer technology and the Internet will assume greater importance for education in the next few years. More courses will be taught online and students will have access to a bewildering and overwhelming range of information, independent of libraries. Some publishers are already looking at contracting with institutions to supply customized electronic packages of course material (for a fee, of course) which students can download as required. Despite this, the traditional library will still be the main support for many courses, but we can use a marriage of traditional and electronic resources to provide better services.

As more institutions perfect their use of interactive video and/or electronic classrooms, "librarians will take a more pro-active role in the classroom and will work more collaboratively with the teaching faculty to develop assignments that are feasible in the off-campus/distant environment.[4] As involvement in developing strong courses for distance delivery increases, the relationship between teaching faculty and librarians will be strengthened. Even now, there are institutions whose contracts for teaching faculty state that they will be expected to teach in both on- and off-campus environments as well as via distance education technologies. As this occurs with more frequency, librarians will become more openly involved with the educational process. "Not only will the increase in distance education bring about greater collaboration between library and teaching faculty, it will bring about greater collaboration among institutions."[5]

In the next few years, the possibility of realizing even greater strides in library service to the extended campus can be anticipated with the economies of scale that will result from state-wise cooperation. Libraries using webpcs will be able to reach out beyond the walls of the institution, expanding exponentially their collections, electronic resources, and expertise. Collectively, libraries will have access to a much larger body of resources that they would have been able to afford and acquire individually. This potential will be more fully realized in the extended campus environment in the next few years.

Two areas that may not change in the next five years are attitudes toward distant learners and mindsets of librarians trained in a non-electronic environment. Some librarians are not prepared to make the leap of the imagination necessary to harness these powerful interactive technologies in creating new service models that capitalize on the new technology, rather than modifying old service models that merely accommodated it. Again, it is important for library educators to take the lead in preparing the next generation of librarians with the vision and sensitivity needed to help tomorrow's off-campus/distant learners become computer and information literate.

## 7. Conclusions

It seems clear that the librarian's role in this context will shift to one of facilitator/instructor, rather than provider of information. It is not difficult to envision a time within the next few years when librarians on campus will be providing real-time assistance to users at remote locations. The capability already exists for a librarian and a remote student to communicate by audio or video conferencing and work simultaneously on the same computer screen. Examples in the cited literature indicate that some libraries are already moving in this direction, although e-mail is currently the most common means of communication in this scenario.[6]

The next few years will see a continuation of traditional off-campus library services combined with a steady growth of student independence in information access. We will also see the rise of commercial information brokers who, for a fee, will deliver customized information to the user's computer or fax machine. These brokers will be in competition with libraries and will appeal to those students who place a high value on their personal time due to family and work responsibilities. Unless motivated otherwise by the educational institution, many students will look for the easiest way possible to obtain information for course purposes. It is up to us as librarians to decide what role we will play in the distance education of the future. In the future, technology will enable libraries to serve distant learners better through networked access and web connectivity. Library schools will need to take the lead here in educating the next generation of librarians, who must be computer literate and sensitized to the special needs of off-campus/distant learners. The curriculum of tomorrow's Library schools will need to reflect a new philosophy of service that is user-oriented rather than library-oriented.

## References

1. Brinkley, Monica, and Jack O'Farrell. "Delivery of Library Services to Distance Education Students: The BIBDEL Research Project at Dublin City University Library." The Electronic Library. v.13, no. 6 (1995): 539-546.
2. Bristow, Ann, and Mary Buechley. "Academic Reference Service Over E-mail: An Update." College & Research Libraries News. v. 56, no. 7 (1995): 459-462.
3. Copeland, Lynn. Review of Library Services for Off-Campus and Distance Education: The Second Annotated Bibliography,

by Alexander L. Slade and Marie A. Kascus. Journal of Distance Education. v. 10, no. 2 (1995): 119-121.

4. Goodson, Carol. "Putting the service back in library service." College & Research Libraries News. v. 58, no. 3 (1997): 186-187.
5. Schiller, Nancy. "World Wide Web Library Support for Distance Learning at the State University of New York at Buffalo." MC Journal: The Journal of Academic Media Librarianship. v. 4, no. 1 (1996): 25-37.
6. Pagell, Ruth A. "The Virtual Reference Librarian: Using Desktop Videoconferening for Distance Reference." The Electronic Library. v. 14, no. 1 (1996): 21-26.

# 5

# Open University System and Library Services : Impact of New Information Technologies

## 1. Introduction

During the past few years the terms "distance learning" and "distance delivery" have gained currency in higher education. They have not been well defined and are often used as synonyms for "distance education, "open learning," web-based learning and "resource based learning". They are also used to suggest certain characteristics including the following: placing the student and learning at the centre of educational paradigm: giving students more autonomy, choice and control by allowing distance starting, finishing and examination times. The approach can be briefly summarised as "what they want, where they want it, when they want it" using, where, possible, available network technologies. Distance delivery can be defined as "the provision of learning and assessment opportunities in modes which serve to increase the degree of student control over when where, how and at what-pace they learns".

Very few universities offer distance learning as described above, but many do offer courses in different modes, thereby, offering some flexibility of choice and taking into account different learning styles. Some of these modes include:

(i) Teaching a course at of-campus sites such as study centre located in other educational organisations and using the facilities provided, or at work places;

(ii) Offering a course in fully external/distance education mode using paper-based forms of delivery, or various electronic forms of delivery such as CD-ROM or Web-based courses as well as other technologies such as video/telephone/electronic conferences;

(iii) Any subject offered may use a combination of these forms;

(iv) An on-campus segment plus go-campus component; and

(v) Various combinations of the above.

Many universities are seeking to offer courses in some form of "place independent" teaching mode. Many cherish the hope that courses will be able to be offered using the Web, thus allowing easy enrolment of students from anywhere. The reality is that there are no "best solutions" to the way courses are delivered. The mode will depend on the student group and its needs, individual learning styles as well as the nature of the course content and association learning objectives. The delivery mediums need also to meet the geographical and on textual needs of the client groups (for example, most of students still do not have easy access to the Internet) and then have the added flexibility to be able to be targeted to a broader market. Equity issues also need to be addressed.

**2. Electronic Resources**

Distance learning students often claim they cannot afford the time necessary to request a book from the library and then wait for it to be delivered through the mail. Libraries have reponded by acquiring multiple copies of books at significant cost to meet the demand from students.

Many instructors prepare books of journal and monograph readings and provide these as part of the materials sent to students. This may result in an expectation that students do not need to read or consult resources beyond the materials provided.

The electronic environment provides opportunities to overcome these problems, if students have network access, then they are able to tap informational resources which are available on the Internet, and can potentially access licensed electronic resources made available from the Library.

### 3. Information Literacy

During the past few years there has been a strong focus on the need for distance learning students to develop information literacy skills. Information literacy is generally understood to include... "the ability to locate, evaluate manage and use information from a range of sources for problem solving, decision making and resear".[1] The library can easily extend the range of assistance it gives to distance learning students by adapting the material it makes available to internal students, keeping in mind always the field of study, the assessment requirements and the background of the student.

### 4. The Library's Changing Role

This has led to a re-examination of the Library's role in relation to distance delivery. The long-term challenge for it is to offer a distinctive product in a rapidly developing marketplace, the immediate challenge for the Library is to provide a service to students which is responsive and innovative and which will assist the University to attract and retain students.

In this context, there will a convergences of off-campus library service with the library's need to serve a growing number of distance learners. Libraries and librarians will have to build new paradigms to serve the many invisible users remotely accessing library catalogues and on-line databases. The extended campus will be a part of every library's future for two reasons;

First, as more emphasis is placed on providing access to information, and less on building collections, the philosophy of library service that required users to come to the library or help and resources will no longer be dominate. Along with the paradigm shift to the electronic library will come the need for a new client-centred philosophy that encompasses remote users and distance learners. Service to the extended campus will become more the norm rather than the exception, and the client-centered service models developed for distant learners will move library service to off-campus and distance education into the forefront.

Second, as technology is used to further library connectivity, we can anticipate significant advances in the delivery of library support to off-campus/distance learners, minimizing the physical disadvantages previously encountered. With more and more academic libraries forming consortia on a state wide basis to provide common access to electronic records, there will be a kaleidoscope of options for distant learners to choose from in terms of Internet and web access, full-text retrieval system, seamless document delivery from published to work station, on-line reference service, and electronic communication. While geographic isolation and social disadvantage can not be wholly eliminated for the distant learner, improvements can be anticipated in this area with existing technological advances. In the present multimedia, interactive, electronic environment, access to instruction and resources is greatly facilitated. "Socialization of students can be accomplished through the use of E-mail, and electronic monitor can help to compensate for the lack of faculty and student face-to-face contact. Electronic chat rooms can further enhance communications among distant learners."[2]

With the aid of powerful interactive technologies and the forging of state wise and regional alliance, education and library support will produce new synergies for cooperation in the absence of walls and institutions. Home librarians, not just off-campus librarians, will serve remote users and distant learners. This convergence will place both on the same trajectory, and distant learners will benefit from the new synergies developed.

For many years, the libraries in western countries have attempted to meet the particular needs of off-campus students. "The Off-campus Support Unit provides a contact point for remote students and assists them to utilise almost the full range of services available to on-campus students. Special services include; book loans; catalogue searches and little recommendations or printed bibliographic, a photocopy delivery service and access to resources at remote study centres."[3]

These libraries also have a long history of addressing the special needs of students undertaking intensive on-campus programs. They have offered extended hours of opening and special orientation programs tailor to the requirements of the students. Facultu librarians have worked closely with the staff of schools offering these programs to maximise the availability of resources for those students who may have very limited opportunity to use the Library because of work and study commitments.

In order for a real partnership to succeed, librarians need to see themselves as part of the teaching and research endeavour, and participate as an active and integral member of the education team. A fundamental tenet of a partnership or collaboration is one of peers working and communicating together. This requires that those involved - librarians, instructional designers and faculty - be equal within the activities and life of the partnership. And this occurs when there is mutual respectfully what each person contributes to the relationship. Peter Drucker states that the "modern organisation....has to be an organisation of equals, of colleagues and associates. No knowledge ranks higher than another, each is judged by its contribution to the common task rather than by an inherent superiority or inferiority."[4]

Where course teams are not the norm the librarians need to approach schools and faculties to convince them of the value of cooperation.

Librarians can make the following types of contributions in course teams;

(i) assisting the course writer(s) in identifying appropriate literature and network resources to support the preparation of the course;

(ii) providing advice about networked electronic resources and internet materials to which students can have access;

(iii) providing information literary components at the course;

(iv) providing advice about the variety of learning resources that may be employed in relation to the place, mode and pace of delivery;

(v) ensuring the staff in the Library known about new products and modes of delivery before student support issues arise;

(vi) Negotiating cost-effective on-line access for students to licensed electronic resources including bibliographic databases as well as full-text databases; and

(vii) information on access to the other learner support services provided by the University or available in the community.

The library needs to monitor the infrastructure requirements involved in the shift to distance delivery and seek involvement in infrastructure development projects, both within the University and within the wider information and telecommunications sector.

As reliable and useful Web sites become available, the Library encourages the use of appropriate Web materials to support courses. The selection skills required build on faculty librarians traditions collection development techniques. Continuity of liaison is important to maintain validity of URLs.

Inducting students into a range of competencies and understandings to enable them to maximise their learning outcomes is a challenging task. Some of the ways in which libraries can responded include the following:

(i) preparation and dissemination of printed guides, help sheets and handbooks adapted, where appropriate for distance learning students;

(ii) provision of electronic tutorials (CD-ROM), Web-Based or floppy discs) using either material prepared for internal students remediable specially a dated for distance learning students;

(iii) special information literary workships held during on-campus schools/workshops, at study centres and/or by video conferences;

(iv) offering for credit a special information literacy unit designed as an intergrate part of a particular course; and,

(v) constantly promoting the essential links between distance delivery modes and the need for information literacy skills.

## 5. Conclusion

In the future, technology will enhance delivery of education and access to libraries making it important to re-examine the standards to insure their reliance to an evolving academic setting. Of libraries, the potential for user-centred, rather than library-centred, service will be enhanced as less emphasis is placed on building collections and more on providing access to resources. In the future, technology will enable libraries to serve distant learners better through networked access and web connectivity. Library schools will need to take the lead here in educating the next generation of libraries, who must be computer literate and sensitized to the special needs of off-campus/ distant learners. The curriculum of tomorrow's library schools will need to reflect a new philosophy of searches that is user-oriented rather than library-oriented. In the next five years, the possibility of realizing even greater strides in library service to the extended campus can be anticipated with the economies of scale that will result from state wise cooperation. Libraries using webpacs will be able to reach out beyond the walls on the institution, expanding exponential their collections, electronic resources, and expertise. Collectively, libraries will have access to a much large body of resources than they would have been able to afford and acquire individually. This potential will be more fully realized in the extended campus environment in the next five years.

Two areas that may not change in the coming years are attitudes toward distant learners and mind sets of librarians trained in a non-electronic environment. Some librarians are not prepared to make the leap of the imagination necessary to harness these powerful interactive technologies in creating new service models that capitalize on the new technology, rather than modifying old service models that merely accommodate it. Again, it is important for library educators to take the lead in preparing the next generation of librarian with the vision and sensitivity needed to help tomorrow's off-campus/distant learners become computer and information literate. Library schools will need to take the lead here in educating the next generation of librarians, who must be computer literate and sensitized to the special needs of off-campus/distant learners. The curriculum of tomorrow's library schools will need to reflect a new philosophy of services that is user-oriented rather than library-oriented.

## References

1. Bruce (C S) & Candy (P C). Developing information literate graduates; prompts for good practice. *In*: D Booker (Ed.), The learning link: Information literacy in practice, Adelaide : Auslib Press, 1995, pp. 245-253.
2. Chalmers (D). Distance delivery at the University of Queensland. *Teaching and Learning News*, 7(2); 1997, pp. 1-2.
3. Creth (S). The electronic library: Toward creating the new information environment (Follett Lecture Series) RL http://www.ukoln.ac.ule/follett/creth/paper.htmt.
4. Drucker (P). Management, New York, Harper Collins, 1997.

# 6

# From Print to Electronic Technologies:
## Implications for Libraries

### 1. Introduction

The medium of print in which text-based information has traditionally been disseminated has shaped one's most fundamental understanding of the nature of text-based discourse and communication. To some extent, that is, terms rooted in the nature of the medium—print products—rather than in the nature of the resource—the intellectual content—shape the discourse. The non-materiality of text-based information as exemplified by the technologies of the late 20th century, in contrast, entails different terms.

Texts are no longer necessarily immutable; rather, they are dynamic. Given that characteristic, interactivity is eminently possible; readers can alter the received texts and reformat the information they contain to suit individual information needs by means of various scanning and sorting mechanisms. Late 20th century technologies, in short, uncouple the material object—the book, the journal, the newspaper—from the intellectual content—the information the material objects contain.

The characteristics of print, therefore, have had profoundly important implications for the storage and dissemination of information, including scholarly information, and thus for the most fundamental aspects of the processes of scholarly activity and communication. The essential distinguishing characteristics of research libraries are themselves expressions of the technology of print, as are those of the various publishing industries that have grown up over the past half millennium. Because printing produces physical objects, libraries, in fulfilling their role as participants in the process of scholarly communication, have accordingly acquired certain fundamental characteristics determined by the nature of the technology and appropriate to the nature of their role in the process of scholarly communication, as currently defined. Libraries have been and continue to be physical space where printed materials are collected, classified, and stored in a way that facilitates access to them. They contain spaces where readers can consult materials in the collection rather than take them elsewhere and the proximity of members of the library staff—specialists in information management—similarly facilitates access.

## 2. Primary and Secondary Texts

One characteristic of electronic information technologies is that they establish a different relationship between interpretive works and the underlying data or primary texts on which they are based. Consider the difference between the more traditional approach to assembling and publishing data and the electronic procedures of for example, Gen Bank, the US national repository for nucleic acid sequence data.[1] In the past scholars and scientists gathered data in an attempt to test a particular hypothesis. When sufficiently important results were obtained, a paper describing them would be published and the authors would typically include some of the data substantiating their conclusions. After electronic databases such as Gen Bank were established, the data contained in such articles would then be extracted and stored electronically. There are limitations inherent in such a model. However, the period between the submission of the manuscript of an article and its publication was inordinately long, and, as the volume of data increased, publishers were understandably reluctant to include anything more than excerpts, especially given that sequence data in printed form was of limited usefulness.

Such a model might apply to humanistic scholarship and scholarly communication as well. Many humanists would be as interested as scientists in having ready access to the full range of primary material underlying scholarly arguments (in this instance, of course, the material is ordinarily different in kind, usually text rather than data). In historical disciplines, for example, one can distinguish between the sources—contemporary chronicles and narrative accounts, letters, diaries, works of art, literature, and music, debit-credit registers, data on demographic trends, government statutes, and so on—and analyses that make use of such material and attempt to package and interpret it in particular ways. It is in the comprehensive assembling of the primary material that electronic information technologies are especially flexible and powerful tools, in part because "the facts are never all in," as Harlan Cleveland has said, and one, therefore, wants to be able to assemble material in a way that is appropriate to the dynamic quality of scholarship, and in part because the new technologies permit one to search the assembled primary material with ease and reorder and reassemble it in ways appropriate to one's purposes.

In the humanities, as in the sciences, many publishers are increasingly unwilling to print lengthy original source material because it is so costly to do so. "[P]rinting costs," wrote the late Eric Cochrane of the University of Chicago, "have all but extinguished the four-century-old tradition of European text editing."[2]

These developments highlight the virtues and limitations of each medium and the appropriateness of particular media to particular material. Electronic media are better suited to storing underlying raw material, whether data or texts. Print, in contrast, is better suited to presenting works of synthesis and interpretation that make use of the raw material. As Henry Riecken has suggested, "It may be no more sensible to publish a commentary on the Miller's Tale in electronic format than to embalm in a printed work the data from the Current Population Survey...."

The example of Gen Bank suggests that, at least in some scientific disciplines, printed journal articles need not contain the documentation for the argument they advance. A more appropriate means to handle documentation might be through reference to the contents of the dynamic electronic database, thus consigning the type of material to the medium that handles it best. One advantage of this approach is that it may lead to shorter, less expensive print products that contain little or no documentation.

Storing the raw material in electronic form, conversely, would in principle permit individual readers to manipulate it in ways that print clearly does not. It also avoids what might be characterised as the compromises and half measures typical of the traditional vehicles of scholarly communication—printed articles that contain the scholarly argument in the main text with brief excerpts from the underlying documentation in footnotes, tables, and appendices.

The new technologies will also permit a fully integrated process in which works of synthesis and interpretation are also published electronically and linked to underlying base data or texts through flexible, sophisticated hypertext and windowing functions, which offer considerable advantages over print in their ability to connect primary and secondary material.

To be sure, various kinds of intellectual material have distinctive characteristics and purposes. But that need not imply that literary or philosophical writing or scholarly works of analysis and interpretation should be exempted from electronic publication in the first instance. It is rather that the arguments for electronic publication of such works are not the same as for substantiating data or documentation. Print continues to be the preferred medium for certain purposes: the printed page is still more readable than a computer screen; a book is more transportable than a portable computer; a subtle argument that unfolds over many "pages" is often more accessible in print than on a computer screen.

### 3. Cost Effectiveness

These are arguments for a print option at some point in the process of scholarly communication because of the advantages that print affords; they are not necessarily arguments for the production of texts, whatever the genre or intellectual purpose, in printed form in the first instance. Even in the case of a commentary on the Miller's Tale, there are advantages to having the text stored electronically, in that a reader can instantly locate a passage in the commentary of particular interest using a search-engine. Electronic media may also be more appropriate media of distribution, with respect to economic cost-effectiveness, in very specialised fields where monographs can, at best, be expected to sell just a few hundred copies.

### 4. Resource Sharing

The availability of text in electronic form has important potential advantages, moreover, for purposes of resource sharing among institutions, in that texts stored electronically are almost instantaneously transmittable. One of the main impediments to resource sharing—the cost and perceived inefficiency of traditional interlibrary loan services—is, therefore, resolvable, at least in principle. Current interlibrary services, which have been described as a bulky process in which a dozen people labour to bring forth a mouse, could be completely transformed. A reader at a university library in California maintained electronically at a library in Massachusetts and decide whether to request that the text be downloaded and printed. A transaction that may take weeks under present circumstances could take seconds, and the reader could choose not to request the text at all after having reviewed a small portion of it.

### 5. Customisation of Information

Electronic storage of text also permits the reader or end-user to tailor universal information to individual needs. McGraw-Hill, has developed a program that permits faculty members at the University of California at San Diego to design their own textbooks[3] they can search an online catalogue from a computer in the university's bookstore for materials in McGraw-Hill's Primis database which contains the full texts of books, journal articles, and so on. The on-site publishing center compiles the materials, creates a title page, and adds an index, table of contents, and page numbers; the entire process can be completed in 48 hours. McGraw-Hill has been granted permission from copyright holders to reprint all materials in the database. Because the texts are created and "published" on demand, faculty members need not anticipate class enrolments weeks or months in advance to order books. More important, faculty members can design texts more precisely suited to their pedagogical purposes. The economic implication of such a capability, as one economist observed, is that largely because of the changes in costs due to electronics, the size of the minimum press run for a title has become smaller. Indeed, McGraw-Hill publishes textbooks on demand from a database of articles or chapters.... The minimum press run is approaching one. The number of titles produced grows in part as titles for narrower audiences become economic.

### 6. Unpublished Research

Electronic publication, finally, has the virtue that it is the only existing medium appropriate for publishing material of certain types, as Jerome Yavarkovsky, Director of the New York State Library, has observed:

> In some instances, research results are not published by conventional, printed means because the results can't be printed and still be meaningful. This is true, for example, when the results are three dimensional, graphic, moving simulations, or animations, or when the outputs are dynamic visual representations of variable processes or theoretical constructs. Traditional, printed publication is completely inadequate for disseminating research of this kind. Yet, this research should be included in what we refer to as "the literature."[4]

### 7. New Paradigms

Because few electronic journals presently exist, no one can confidently predict what new paradigms of scholarly communication in the electronic age will eventually emerge. Our objective in this section is simply to offer a few suggestions as to how scholarly publication might work.

It is critical that in starting virtually "from scratch" with a brand new "making public" vehicle, we are unfettered by old modes of viewing and doing publishing: by existing notions of publishing offices; marginal cost structure of publishing; the idea of "circulation;" indexing and abstracting; "monographs" and "serials;" advertising; ownership; possibly even profits. We have the opportunity to begin with a blank page—even that notion needs a new metaphor.[5]

### 8. Electronic Production and Distribution

Assuming that the principal current document formats—monographs and periodicals—will continue to exist in an electronic environment, at least for a time, the new technologies will no doubt first be applied to the tasks of producing and distributing traditional kinds of documents.[6] Let us begin with production.

When a scholar finishes the manuscript of a journal article and sends it to a publisher, it is ordinarily subjected to editorial and peer review. Some observers have suggested that the traditional editorial and peer review processes might be circumvented altogether because electronic information technologies so facilitate communication among scholars. In Henry Riecken's words, a jaundiced view might hold that desktop publishing suffers from the same blight as computer network 'bulletin boards'—anyone with the equipment can 'publish' whatever he wants, of whatever merit or interest, and the potential audience is left with the task of sifting through the midden.

However, the new technologies may well expand the review process and change its character, with preliminary versions of manuscripts being made available on a network for comment by interested readers. The author would then prepare a final version, incorporating any suggestions that seem to have particular merit.[7] Even if this expanded process does not develop, the traditional one is greatly expedited in an electronic environment. Editors can send manuscripts to reviewers and receive responses much more quickly, thus reducing the period between the time of the manuscript's submission and editorial decisions.[8]

The manuscript then goes into production, and here electronic technologies have already been effectively employed. If the author has submitted his or her text in electronic form, the cost of original typesetting is considerably lower, since the compositor's task is simply to edit the electronic version of the text, and original keying of characters is kept to a minimum. Both author and editor can have changes made readily, using global search and change functions.

Whether the new technologies will result in other significant production cost savings is difficult to determine at this point. Many of the principal costs have less to do with the medium than with the nature of the activity. For example, many of the costs associated with the highly labor-intensive editorial and peer review processes will remain, while some costs associated with the actual production of the text—typesetting, in particular—can almost certainly be reduced.

Once author and editor have settle upon a final version of the text, it is distributed. Traditionally, distribution has consisted of shipping or mailing printed and bound copies of the first copy to individuals, vendors and libraries. In an electronic environment there might be a variety of distribution media. Publishers might continue to make hard copy available on demand from their own printers to clients who do not yet have the means to make use of electronic versions of texts (or prefer paper). Alternatively, they might issue titles on CD-ROM or floppy disc; these have an advantage over printed volumes in that they miniaturise the text, so that the considerable space problems libraries face might be addressed by this kind of distribution.[9] Such products might either be sold to the user, whether individual or institutional, or leased. In either case, the option to download and print the text or any portion thereof might be controlled by the sales or rental agreement. If the CD-ROM or floppy disc is sold or leased to an institution, the publisher might also specify in the agreement that the text is not to be mounted on a local-area network, so that more than one reader can have access to it simultaneously.[10] In any of these cases, the cost of printing, if it is permitted could be the responsibility of the individual user, just as now the individual ordinarily incurs the cost of photocopying printed material in a library's collection.

The option that appears to be of unusual interest is that texts will be mounted on a local-area or wide-area network and clients provided with direct access to them online. Under such circumstances one can envision a variety of retrieval architectures. Individual institutions—colleges and universities—might choose to maintain local electronic repositories of frequently used titles they had purchased outright from the publishers; in that case the cost of the telecommunications connection with the publishers would be eliminated. Alternatively, some publishers might choose not to sell titles but rather maintain them at central sites themselves and charge users on a fee-per-use basis. Yet a third kind of architecture may eventually evolve in which libraries at different institutions collaborate in collecting electronic materials; under those circumstances the consortium will own a full complement of resources but will distribute them among the different members of the consortium.

### 9. Publication Costs

To what extent any of these methods of distribution will result in cost savings is difficult to determine now with any precision. Any of them could have significant positive implications for libraries' space problems, as we have suggested, although there will continue to be substantial costs associated with storage, especially if texts are maintained in online databases. William Y. Arms suggests that "[t]oday, storing a document on a computer is more expensive than on paper, but prices are falling rapidly. By the end of the decade, online computing will be much cheaper than storing books.

### 10. Distribution Costs

There are other costs entailed in distribution. Let us consider, for example, a journal published by a university press that is currently mailed to subscribers; if the texts of the articles are instead mounted at the university's BITNET node and subscribers elsewhere retrieve them from the network, the cost of mailing, currently recovered in the subscription price, is eliminated, as are the costs of printing and binding on the publisher's part. On the other hand, both the university where the journal is produced and the university where it is received incur costs associated with the operation of the computing and telecommunications facilities supporting the electronic distribution; such costs are ordinarily hidden, at least from the individual subscriber, yet they, nonetheless, exist. How the costs for various phases of the process of scholarly communication in a fully electronic environment will compare to those incurred now is clearly a subject for considerable further investigation, as is the associated question of who will absorb which costs.

Now let us consider some of the possibilities inherent in these various options. First, individual readers could tailor the information to particular needs. The reader might be able to excerpt and print a single chapter (or page) of a monograph or a single article of a journal issue. Indeed, as several observers have suggested, the very concept of an issue of a journal is challenged by electronic information technologies.[12] Articles are currently collected together and an issue published when there is a sufficient number of articles available to make up an issue. In an electronic environment, one can envision a situation where a single article will be mounted on a network as soon as it clears editorial review; there will be no need to wait for other articles to reach the same point in the process. It is in this sense that some of the distinctions entailed by the technology of print invite reconsideration.

## 11. Subscription and Pricing Patterns

Precisely because electronic technologies permit individual information needs to be met, different subscription and pricing schemes and practices will almost surely develop, whether for individuals or institutions. For example, publishers or vendors would presumably be able to charge on the basis of the amount of material retrieved: the entire text of a monograph or any part thereof, an individual journal article, a page or even a few paragraphs of material downloaded selectively. Case Western Reserve University and IBM are attempting to monitor this process within the university through a software that functions as a kind of royalties manager. On a larger scale CitaDel, the new citation and document-delivery service of the Research Libraries Group, allows for online ordering, delivering, and billing.

Publishers, moreover, may choose to offer various services of other kinds. Although many subscribers will wish to continue to receive routinely all the articles published in a particular journal, it will be possible for publishers to facilitate selective acquisition as well. A comprehensive, fully integrated service could provide tables of contents, lists of article titles, or abstracts of periodical articles or monographs, as INFO-SOUTH now begins to do for Latin American studies. Prospective buyers could skim portions of a full text on a read-only, not-keep basis. Readers could order individual items of interest by means of a simple command; the document could then be delivered by any number of methods.

## 12. Publishers and Librarians: Redefining the Roles

Some redefinition of the traditional roles of publisher, vendor, and library and of the relationships among them is almost inevitable. Because individual end-users will be able to purchase information tailored specifically to their needs, they will perhaps be more inclined to interact directly with publishers or vendors—that is, readers may not need to rely as much on the library. Libraries, for their part, may develop a different approach to acquiring materials, more appropriate to the characteristics of electronic technologies. Such an approach has been termed the "just-in-time" model, as constrasted with the "just-in-case" model currently governing libraries' acquisition practices. Because libraries will ultimately have ready access to electronic versions of texts stored elsewhere, they will be able to base acquisition practices on immediate reader needs rather than on a priori assumptions about what those needs might be. Instead of subscribing to a certain number of journals, for example, libraries may instead negotiate contracts for a certain number of discrete articles from a national database of articles, acquired in response to readers' requests.

It also seems clear that there may be some blurring in the distinctions among the historical roles of publishers as producers, vendors as intermediaries, and librarians as archivists. Scholarly publishers have traditionally allowed titles to go out of print because of libraries, willingness to serve as a sort of secondary distribution system and warehouse. The costs associated with archiving materials have been the responsibility of the library. In an electronic environment, where texts can be miniaturized and storage costs greatly reduced, publishers and vendors may be more inclined to maintain archives of texts for many years.

It may also be that traditional models of resource sharing among libraries will be affected. Libraries have historically turned to other libraries for materials not owned locally; if such materials continue to be available from publishers or vendors, libraries might be inclined to acquire them directly, if resources permit and the demand justifies acquisition. Under any of these circumstances, the rapidly changing state of the technology is likely to be an important dynamic. As Jerome Yavarkovsky suggested, "A necessary feature of online accessibility and network publishing is a commitment to archival storage. Once an article is accepted and published online, the publisher, or some other agency, must keep that publication available in perpetuity, in the same way that traditional publications are held permanently by research libraries. This archival responsibility might even be one of the roles possible for research libraries in the future."

## 13. Changes in Scholarly Ethos and Communication

Electronic information technologies may, some observers think, bring about far more significant changes. Indeed, some envision fundamental changes in scholarly ethos and practices of scholarly communication as a result of their introduction. Apart from the expanded processes of peer review described earlier, the new technologies could permit immediate and public response from reader to electronic publications and allow them access to the reactions of prior readers. Further, since their invention centuries ago, footnotes and bibliographic references have connected texts to prior pertinent writings and documented the arguments authors wish to advance. As such, they serve as print equivalents of hypertext. But the analogy is far from perfect. Footnotes and bibliographic references are always selected samples of the full range of material that might be related to the text at issue. Electronic technologies such as hypertext permit access to a much wider range of relevant materials—both primary and secondary, substantiating and contradictory—than those authors have elected to call to readers' attention. In this new environment, readers need not rely on authors' selective presentations of related materials and can, if they choose, seek additional references for themselves using electronic media.

These new technologies may also permit the emergence of new institutions or infrastructures supporting scholarly communication. The advent of electronic capabilities provides the university with the potential for becoming the primary publisher in the scholarly communication process. At the present, we are in the untenable position of generating knowledge, giving it away to the commercial publisher, and then buying it back for our scholars at increasingly prohibitive prices. The electronic revolution provides the potential for developing university controlled publishing enterprises through scholarly networks supported either by individual institutions or consortia.

How might such a system function? One proponent envisions two broad types of campus network nodes, editorial and distributing. The first of these would offer editorial software for creating and reviewing papers. As demand dictated, it might also store publications held by an editorial node at another campus, a redundancy that would reduce telecommunications costs and network traffic. The second type of node would exist solely to distribute publications by making them accessible online and would resemble traditional libraries by serving as repositories of publications created and issued elsewhere. The distinction expressed in this scenario is familiar and approximates the distinction between the collecting or archiving function currently performed by libraries and the production function performed by university presses. In the new environment, librarians might continue to be responsible for decisions about which materials are made directly available to local readers. Access to materials stored elsewhere, however, might well be more directly controlled by the individual reader than in the case under the terms of current interlibrary loan services.

A variety of pricing and compensation schemes, similar to those anticipated earlier, might emerge: a licensing fee paid to a particular publisher might permit a local node to provide access to all the publisher's works: subscription fees might be based on anticipated use of subsets of a node's publications, with users—institutions or individuals—paying for access to parts of the node's holdings; alternatively, access might be on a fee-per-use basis. For individual institutions, there will continue to be important and difficult questions to resolve concerning the extent to which the costs of these services are assumed by the institution or passed off to the individual user.

One can envision how the system might operate. Individual scholars interested in accessing particular titles at their own workstations might first determine whether the titles were among those purchased by their institutions and loaded at the local campus network node. If the texts were available locally, the individual readers might be able to access them on a read-only basis, just as now they access printed materials in the university library on a read-only basis. If they chose to download and print portions of the text retrieved, they might be expected to assume some of the cost of doing so, just as now they asume the cost of photocopying printed material. If the text were not available locally, they might be able to scan the first few panels of text on a read-only, not-keep basis by means of a telecommunications connection, either with the publisher's (editorial) node or with the distributing node at another campus within the consortium (in this instance, the local library or its descendant institution might continue to act as mediator in the process). If they decided, once again, to retrieve and print all or part of the text, they might be charged according to whether the title was acquired directly from the publisher or from a fellow member of the consortium.

What any of these scenarios might permit is an assertion (or reassertion) of the university's direct role in scholarly communication. The commercial publishers entered the market because they offered economies of scale and technical expertise to professional societies interested in publishing conference proceedings and professional papers. To a considerable extent these new technologies may eventually obviate the need to rely so much on the commercial publishers for their expertise, especially since many of those involved in editorial work for learned journals, even those published by commercial publishers, are academics with university appointments: copyright, if it remains in force in anything like its present form, can be held either by the author or the sponsoring university.

## 14. Issues to be Resolved: Adulteration of Text, Functioning of the Network

Clearly, a number of issues must be successfully addressed and resolved by all the relevant parties before electronic technologies, whatever their virtues, will be seen as preferable to print as a medium of distribution. There is, first, the question of ensuring the authenticity and integrity of the text. "Electronic text," Riecken notes, is far more susceptible to distortion, adulteration, and mischievous or criminal alteration than printed pages. Text on CD-ROMs (read-only memory discs) cannot be changed and thereby prevent alterations of the sort that concern Riecken.

The very characteristic of electronic text that permits easy adulteration is in another way a source of concern to publishers, and in what follows here we are anticipating some of the substance of the later discussion on copyright. A technology (photocoyping) already exists that provides prospective buyers of a printed media product with an alternative to buying it (although a less satisfactory one). Anyone who would otherwise subscribe to a journal who instead photocopies selected articles of interest takes advantage of an existing technology to avoid subscribing, and the publisher is denied revenue.

Publishers are understandably concerned that making texts of scholarly material available electronically will greatly facilitate this kind of circumvention. Publishers of computer software programs, for example, are aware that there are a great many pirate copies of their products. Their response is to change substantially for every copy legitimately sold to offset the economic effects of illegal copying just as University Microfilms does for photocopies of journal articles.

It will be important, moreover, to refine and extend electronic access functions approximating the kind of intellectual activity occurring when a scholar browses in a library or skims the pages of a learned journal. When the latest issue of a core journal in a particular discipline is published, many scholars at least skim the opening pages of articles outside their own subspecialty to have some sense of what colleagues are writing about generally in the discipline. If one had to retrieve the text of the latest issue from a network, would one be more inclined to retrieve and print only the articles in one's own subspecialty? Would one's own interests become ever narrower as a result? As suggested, a related issue concerns the ability to browse in a library.

Some interesting discoveries are made serendipitously; will scholars be able to make such discoveries as easily in an electronic environment?

Illustrative material—black-and-white or colour reproductions or works of art or other images, graphs, and charts—presents particular problems, which may explain why, until very recently, there was not a single peer-reviewed electronic journal in the sciences, where scholars make extensive use of such material. It is certainly technologically possible to offer such material and with fully satisfactory results; the issue is rather that to do so assumes the availability of specific equipment and software. There are not yet universally accepted conventions for representing images digitally, and the inconsistent methods of representing and resolving such information are an added complexity.

Finally, there are many questions to be resolved concerning the functioning of the network and the principles governing scholarly publication therein. Among them are issues of availability, affordability, and friendly access : the consequences of a shift from the current subsidisation of the network to its eventual commercialisation; intellectual standards (the integrity of texts and privacy); underlying cost structure (cost recovery, methods of collecting and distributing revenues, and so on); ownership and copyright practices; and academic culture (incentives or disincentives associated with publishing one's work on the network instead of by traditional means). In the culture of print, the fundamental issues of this type were addressed and resolved many years ago, and paradigms governing scholarly practices and the functioning of the entire system, with all its complexities, have been widely accepted. The new technologies provoke fundamental reconsideration.

The various scenarios sketched here suggest both the potential and flexibility of electronic technologies and also some of their current limitations. It is likely that the electronic information technologies of the late 21st century will be utilised in this way for some time; eventually, their distinctive characteristics will almost certainly produce fundamentally different kinds of genres.

Perhaps the most important characteristic of electronic information technologies that will serve to produce a new kind of writing is precisely that the technologies permit almost instantaneous communication. The fact that the technology of print often entails an extended process from the time a manuscript is submitted to its publication may perhaps be related, though not in an uncomplicated way, to the deep meanings, ambiguities, and complex structures characteristic of print genres; electronic technologies, conversely, encourage the communication of fresh, immediate observations.

## 15. Conclusion

These initiatives present challenges to library staff members and others involved in providing information services to the members of an academic community. Among them are issues of selection (including the matter of simply being aware of the existence of particular electronic journals), acquisition (knowing the correct subscription information and successfully placing orders and retrieving and downloading the texts), cataloging (providing readers with adequate access information, including information about the medium, how one subscribes, how one specifies the "location" of electronic materials within the "collection") access and retrieval (including "adding value," such as the possibility of doing keyword or simple string searches of the ASCII text), indexing of contents, archiving, and so on.

Various initiatives at a number of institutions are likely to yield lessons of value to many others. At Carnegie Mellon University, the Mercury Electronic Library now stores information sources of various types, including the page images of the journals included in Elsevier's TULIP program. These can be read online over the campus network. The key feature of CMU's practical success is the early adoption of a distributed approach to computing—that is, acceptance of diverse types of workstations and formats for the storage of information, as well as of the concept of dispersed storage of information.

More important than the differences among these projects is their common assumption that the roles of the component institutions in the process of scholarly communication are changing and in ways that can be understood only by practical attempts to discover what is effective.

## References

1. Burks, Christian: Cinkoksy, Michael J. (1991). Electronic data publishing and gen bank," *Science* 252. 1273-77.
2. Cochrane, Eric. (1981). Historians and Historiography in the Italian Renaissance. Chicago, The University of Chicago Press, 1981, Pp xv+295.
3. Riecken, Henry W. Scholarly publication: Are there viable options?" Draft for the Research Library Committee of the Council on Library Resources (US) 1989, 16, 18.
4. Yavarkovsky, Jerome. (1990). A University-based electronic publishing network," *EDUCOM Review* 25 (1990): 14-20.

5. Okerson, Ann (1992). "Scholarly Publishing and Technologies," *Scholarly Publishing* 23, 1-4.
6. Yavarkovsky, Jerome. University-based Electronic Publishing Network," 19; Riecken, *Scholarly Publication*, 13.
7. Arms, William Y. (1992). Scholarly publishing on the national networks," *Scholarly Publishing* 23 : 158-69.
8. Pagell, Ruth A. (1996). The Virtual Reference Librarian: Using Desktop Videoconferencing for Distance Reference." *The Electronic Library* 14, 1: 21-26.
9. Wynne, Peter M. (1996) Experimentation with electronic document delivery in the BIBDEL Project at the University of Central Lancashire." *The Electronic Library* 14, 1:13-20.
10. *Ibid*.
11. Battin, "Library: Center of the Restructured University," 175. See also Ann Okerson Back to academia? The case for American universities to publish their own research," *LOGOS* 2: 106-12.
12. *Ibid*, 18.

# 7

# Designing Web Based Learning Modules for People with Special Needs : Some Guidelines and Practices

## 1. Introduction

Participants in online activities include an increasing group of users with sensory, physical or learning disabilities, for whom adaptive technologies provide a gateway to information and education. Current estimates suggest that approximately 20% of the population have some type of disability.[1] Legislation in developed countries supports development of accessible standards for Web-based resource development. Furthermore, today's technological environment is fostering public demand for accommodation of a growing number of user interface models, ranging from screen readers to palm pilots to telephone browsers. All of these point to the need for Web authors to increase their understanding of the principles and practices which support universal design.

## 2. Universal Design Principles

Why should developers take the time to ensure that Web-based educational resources are based on universal design principles? There are several factors that should motivate us to learn about accessible design, and implement it in our online programming. The first is a fundamental ideas that access to education is one of our basic human rights. Accommodation of learners with special needs is part of the process of ensuring that high quality educational experiences are available to every individual.

We are currently in the midst of a rapid evolution in availability of adaptive technology that removes barriers to accessing information and education for people with disabilities. A potential learner may have differences in how they interact with a computer, including both hardware and software, input and output. A sensory impairment may result in a need to use screen reader software to hear the information instead of viewing it on a screen. Limitations in mobility could mean that the student uses an adapted keyboard to navigate the Web. However, these individuals are fully capable to participating and contributing to a learning community. Education delivered via the Internet provides an opportunity to level the playing field for learners with special needs through use of new technologies, in combination with thoughtful design of the user interface. The technology is available, but the onus now rests with designers to present Web-based resources in formats that are accessible to a full range of learners. As an extension of the principle of universal education, we must become aware of principles of universal Web design.

At present, the leader in establishing accessibility guidelines for page authoring is the Web Accessibility Initiative (WAI), a sub-committee of the World Wide Web Consortium (W3C).[1] The mission of this group includes promotion of a high degree of usability for people with disabilities. To this end, the WAI is coordinating many organisations that have developed a comprehensive and unified set of accessibility guidelines. The most recent set of authoring guidelines categories, by priority, elements and formats to a void and recommends possible redundancies or alternatives, in an attempt to establish universal standards for accessible Web design.[2]

**3. Legislation**

In several countries the Human Rights Code protects citizens against any "discriminatory practice in the provision of goods, services, facilities or accommodation customarily available to the general public."[3]

In the US, the Americans with Disabilities Act (ADA)[4] legislation and the Rehabilitation Act 508 requirements for Federal Departments and Agencies require that Web resources must be made accessible to people with disabilities. The ADA directs organisations falling within its scope to provide appropriate auxiliary aids and services where necessary to ensure effective communication with individuals with disabilities, unless doing so would result in a fundamental alteration to the programme or service or is an undue burden.

**4. Reaching the Widest Possible Audience**

In the field of education, we are all experiencing the exponentially increasing demand for provision of course related resources and documents via the Internet. Use of the Web for delivery of distance learning is finding an audience in the current "just-in-time" education environment, where customised programs and convenient professional development opportunities are valued by today's lifelong learners. In addition, students in traditional facilities-based courses are asking for the convenience of access to course resources, information, and communication with their instructors via the Internet. Library reference services are being adapted to take advantage of the possibility of Internet access to information systems and database mining tools.

We may have an image in mind of a "typical" learner, who sits at a desk using a conventional keyboard, mouse and monitor. But it is important to consider demographic trends, health trends and technological trends, to ensure that we are reaching the widest possible audience. An aging population, in combination with the demand for lifelong learning, has lead to an increase in the number of users who have some degree of vision impairment. Additionally, workplace environments have unfortunately resulted in a dramatic increase in the number of learners who suffer from repetitive strain injury.

The potential benefits of Web-based learning resources for students who use adaptive technologies are many, as the electronic delivery of information and resources permits translation into a variety of modalities and formats. These benefits include:

(i) flexibility in the pace of learning, material can be presented in redundant, reinforcing or alternative formats *e.g.*, (ii) speech, print, graphics, etc.; material can be adapted to various learning styles; student can clarify, rehearse and review supporting materials without (iii) interrupting the flow of the learning session for classmates; issues of distance, transportation and physical accessibility are reduced, (iv) equal participation for students who use augmentative or alternative; (v) communication methods, as the method and rate of communication is (vi) transparent to fellow classmates; and greater opportunities for peer interaction and collaboration, and for (vii) student-instructor interaction and assistance.

Another trend is the rapid development of alternative devices such as mobile computing devices, "hands-free" and "eyes-free" browsers and "virtual books" to access information and resources in contexts other than the conventional desktop workstation. Not all mehods of accessing the Web incorporate a graphical pointing device such as a mouse. Web pages based on principles of accessible design should be navigable via keyboard or voice commands. While the functionality of these devices is determined by the product developers, strategies may be inplemented to enhance access and avoid unnecessary barriers being created.

Forward thinking developers will recognise the need to plan for changes linked to demographic and technological trends. To this end, it is essential that educators and administrators are astute in their design of Web-based instructional resources, and in their selection of courseware tools. Building on a solid foundation which includes adherence to HTML standards and accommodation of a full range of interface models will increase the life span of the resources we develop, ensuring access by the widest possible audience at present, and in the future.

## 5. Accessible Design: Where Does it Begin?

A useful definition of accessibility is provided by Chuck LeTourneau, of Starling Web Services, an organisation that specialises in accessible Web design. He states:

"What does 'Web accessibility' mean? To me, it means that anyone using any kind of Web browsing technology must be able to visit any site and get a full and complete understanding of the information as well as have the full and complete ability to interact with the site - if that is necessary"[5].

In order to understand the issues related to accessible Web design, developers need to first have a basic understanding of specific access systems that accommodate, replace or augment sensory and motor functions of users with special needs. These include voice recognition systems, alternative pointing devices. screen readers/magnifiers, and other devices. The following is a list of some adaptive technologies and examples of basic challenges to Internet navigation faced by users of these devices.

### 5.1 *Screen Readers*

This software is used by blind learners to access Web pages, electronic text and computer applications. This software allows all text to be read out from the menu, toolbar and directory buttons, and Web pages. Tab or Shift-Tab allows navigation through the Hyperlinks on a given page.

### 5.2 *Screen Magnifiers*

Screen magnification systems enlarge portions of the screen to allow learners with limited vision to access computer based materials.

### 5.3 *Alternative Keyboards*

These keyboards offer larger or smaller target areas for users with loss of gross or fine motor control. They may be switched to mouse emulation mode so that the arrow keys or numeric keypad of the same keyboard are used for mouse movements.

Mouse emulation can be somewhat slow or frustrating, although keyboard equivalents to tab through hypertext links which have been built into recent Web browsers are very helpful. Because the pointing device is less precise, users may need larger targets or increased spacing between targets.

### 5.4 *On-screen Keyboards*

This software allows the user to enter text and select buttons emulating menu functions from a display on the monitor. Users have a pointing device or a switch to select buttons.

### 5.5 *Voice Recognition*

The user speaks into a microphone to navigate software applications, surf the Web, and input text. Commands correlating to macro sequences may be created to customise usage for specific software or frequent tasks. Mouse control may incorporate a grid system.

A basic understanding of these commonly used adaptive technologies, is the first step in learning to design

Web pages that will make information accessible to users of these adaptive technologies.

### 6. Best Practices for Accessible Design

Making the Web more accessible is largely dependent upon using HTML the way it was intended: to encode meaning and structure, rather than control layout and visual formatting. Some years ago, the introduction of graphical browsers, lead to a variety of new official and unofficial HTML formats which were quickly taken up by Web designers. Adaptation of the structure of HTML for aesthetic purposes compromises the accessibility of the site using non-visual, or non-conventional browsers. An example of this phenomenon is the case of the Table tag that was originally conceived to display tabular data, but has become an all-purpose tool for lying out magazine-type pages. The increasing use of graphics, non-standard HTML structure, and the introduction of dynamic elements such as Java applets and active-X controls has further compounded the challenges in designing universally accessible Web pages.

### 7. General Principles

Knowledge of the following general principles, based on WAI approach to accessible design will help the designer to achieve greater level of accessibility in the learning resources being developed.

#### 7.1 *Use structural elements as they were intended*

One of the greatest barriers to accessibility is inappropriate use of structural markup to achieve visual formatting effects. Using markup improperly may create a barrier preventing users with specialised software from understanding the organisation of a page, and navigating through it effectively. Web designers may be tempted to use structural markup to achieve a desired formatting effect, especially for viewing with older browsers. Common practices include use of tables for layout or a header to change the font size. It is important to consider whether the formatting effect is so critical as to warrant rendering the page inaccessible to some users. Not everyone uses a conventional monitor and mouse to access the Web. A better approach is to use markup such as TABLE, UL, BLOCKQUOTE, etc. as it was intended, and use CSS to format visual effects for those learners using conventional desktop system. CSS is a forward thinking technology that assists the Web designer in separating structure from format, content from presentation. This accommodates users of adaptive technology, as well as users of new, mobile and portable Internet access devices.

### 7.2 *Provide equivalent alternatives to auditory and visual content*

When providing critical information in strictly visual, or auditory formats, be certain to include alternatives for those learners who may not be able to access these resources. A simple example is the use of the "ALT" attribute, of the <IMG> tag, providing an alternative text for users who are not displaying graphics. This will accommodate learners accessing Web resources with a screen reader, with graphics turned off because of low bandwidth issues, or those who are using devices which display text only. Scripts, sound files, objects, java applets, and other interactive components should also be rendered in alternative formats.

### 7.3 *Add accessibility features to ensure pages can be navigated by keyboard only*

As not all users can use, or will be using a mouse to navigate Web pages, good Web design means that the page can be accessed using only a keyboard or voice commands. Common pitfalls include use of image maps without ALT tags for each "hotspot." You can also use HTML 4.0 features such as ACCESSKEY and TABINDEX to make your pages easier to navigate using only a keyboard.

### 7.4 *Ensure graceful transformation*

With some effort, Web designers can create pages that transform gracefully. Pages that transform gracefully will be accessible to a variety of users despite any physical, sensory, and cognitive disabilities, work constraints, and technological barriers. Strategies already mentioned include separation of structure from format, providing textual as well as visual information, and creation of documents that do not rely on one type of browser or hardware. Pages should be usable by people using a keyboard, with small or low resolution screens, black and white screens, no screens, with only voice or text output, etc.

## 8. Basic strategies to ensure Accessible Design

With so many tools available, one is easily tempted to implement design elements that in the end may actually impede, rather than enhance, the learning process for computer users with special needs. The following tips, based on the Web Accessibility Initiative guidelines, will assist in ensuring that your Web site is reaching the widest possible audience.

### 8.1 *Images and animations*

Use the alt attribute to describe the function of all visuals. Since text content can be presented to the user as synthesised speech, braille, and visually-displayed text, this improves accessibility for people who cannot access visual information or written text, including many individuals with blindness, cognitive disabilities, learning disabilities, and deafness.

### 8.2 *Image maps*

Use client-side MAP and text for hotspots. Client-side image maps are preferable because information is located in the HTML document and can be accessed using alternative browsers. Server-side image maps may require use of a mouse or other pointing device. Text equivalents are helpful for the reasons outlined above.

### 8.3 *Multimedia*

Provide captioning and transcripts of audio, descriptions of video, and accessible versions in case inaccessible formats are used. Although some people cannot use movies, sounds, audio enhancements, etc. directly, they may still use pages that include equivalent textual information to the visual or auditory content.

### 8.4 *Hypertext links*

Use text that makes sense when read out of context. Link text should be meaningful enough to make sense when read out of context — either on its own or as part of a sequence of links. For instance, do not use "click here." Link text should also be terse.

### 8.5 *Page organisation*

Use headings, lists, and consistent structure. Use CSS for layout and style where possible.

Use structural markup to aid navigation rather than for a presentation effect (e.g., using a table for layout or a header to change the font size). Correct use helps learners with specialised software to understand the organisation of the page and to navigate through it.

### 8.6 *Tables*

Make line by line reading sensible. Summarise. Avoid using tables for column layout.

Tables used to lay out pages and some data tables where cell text wraps pose problems for older screen readers that do not interpret the source HTML or browsers that do not allow navigation of individual table cells. These screen readers will read across the page, reading sentences on the same row from different columns as one sentence.

### 8.7 *Choosing Courseware Tools*

An exponentially increasing number of educational courses, from all sectors, are being offered over the Web.

This has spurred a growing industry of software tools to assist in creation of Web-based curriculum and in performing class management tasks. Web server software such as WebCT, Top Class, CourseInfo, Virtual-U and other programs will take HTML documents, along with other media and resources, and quickly organise them into a framework specifically designed for delivery of Web-based courses.

Courseware products cater to educators who are unfamiliar with programming, allowing easy integration of password protection, interactive activities, tracking of student progress, etc. Generally, the interface is fairly simple for the designer, as many use templates and wisards extensively to assist in course content creation. Step-by-step guides support creation of a range of components, from the course home page, to bulletin boards, to quisses and marking systems. Multimedia components, such as images or audio files, are generally created externally in a specialised software program, and imported. Many feature a designer interface which is driven by a program residing on the server, accessed through a browser. While this is convenient in terms of software access and cross platform issues, the automation can give the educator less control of the final formatting of the HTML.

Thus, while Web-based distance education programs built on courseware platforms address geographical and cost barriers, they frequently present access barriers to students with special needs. Ironically, very few include basic accessibility features described above, effectively excluding those individuals who stand to benefit most from new technologies.

## 9. Conclusion

Looking at the future of computer interface and emerging technologies the motivators behind development of accessible Web-based learning resources are many.

Improving accessibility begins with increased awareness of the potential barriers. As educators, we must be astute in selection of courseware tools and encourage use of products and methods that allow development of accessible resources based on principles of universal access. Just as wheelchair ramps to buildings have become the norm in architectural design, accessible Web design must become a basic consideration in the design of Web-based learning resources.

## References

1. Web Accessibility Initiative (W3C) Web Content Accessibility Guidelines 1.0, 5-May-1999. Retrieved July 1999 from the WWW:, http://www.w3.org/TR/WAI-WEBCONTENT/
2. Canadian Human Rights Act. July 1999 WWW: http://www.chrc.ca/chra-lcdp
3. LeTourneau, C. (1998) WAI-IG List Serve Archive re: Canadian Government and Web accessibility. WWW: http://lists.w3.org/Archives/Public/w3c-wai-eo/1998OctDec/0061.html.
4. Treviranus, J. (1998). Future Trends, Emerging Technologies and Students with Special Needs. *In : Proceedings of SETTT Conference held in proceedings, Toronto, Ontario, 1998* http://www.utoronto.ca/atrc/rd/slideshows/future/index.htm
5. ATRC Staff. Alternative Keyboard and Other Enhancements. WWW:http://www.utoronto.ca/atrc/reference/tech/altkey.html

# 8

# Selection Criteria for Quality Controlled Information Gateways

## 1. Introduction

Internet subject gateways have mostly defined 'quality' with relation to carefully chosen lists of selection criteria. Quality has, however, been a subject of serious study in industry and management science since the World War II. It might be useful to describe some of the concepts developed by management theorists and practitioners and to investigate their relevance to the quality selection issue. Finally, work being done on databases and information quality will be described.

## 2. Concept of Quality in Industry and Management Science

Quality has been analysed as a factor in the management process since the 1930s, but it was not until after the World War II that it became important. North American managers brought in to advise Japanese companies on restructuring after the war and devised new concepts of quality which began to be universally accepted. The important pioneers in this field were W. Edwards Deming, Joseph M. Juran and Kaoru Ishikawa.

A universally agreed definition of quality still does not exist. Juran[1] suggested that quality should be seen as 'fitness for use'. Another short definition views quality as 'conformance to requirements' rather than 'goodness, or luxury, or shininess, or weight'.[2] These definitions from the management literature make it clear that quality cannot just be defined in relation to some abstract concept of 'excellence', but should be seen in relation to the demands of the user of the final product. A recent working definition of 'quality' has been provided by Clark.[3] 'How consistently the product or service delivered, meets or exceeds the customers' (external and internal) expectations and needs.'

In the management context, quality processed can be applied to any product. A product can be defined as the 'output of any process', consisting mainly of 'goods, software, and services'.

### 2.1 *Product Quality*

Product quality is usually defined with specific relation to the product, whether it is a goods or services. For goods, important aspects might be reliability, durability, performance characteristics, aesthetics, etc. These dimensions will differ according to the product type: the most important factor being whether it meets the end requirements of the customer.

### 2.2 *Service Quality*

Early quality models concentrated on goods. The enormous growth of the service sector in Western economies since the World War II has resulted in a growing literature on service quality. Defining and modelling the quality of services is generally acknowledged to be more difficult than modelling the quality of goods due to the intangible nature of services themselves. There are two popular models of services quality in use.

### 2.3 *Gronroos's Service Quality Model*

The model created by Gronroos[4] attempts to understand how the quality of a given service is perceived by customers.

It divides the customer's perception of any particular service into two dimensions:

(i) Technical quality: What the consumer receives, the technical outcome of the process.

(ii) Functional quality: How the consumer receives the technical outcome, what Gronroos calls the "expressive performance of a service".

Gronroos suggested that, in the context of services, functional quality is generally perceived to be more important than technical quality, assuming that the service is provided at a technically satisfactory level. He also points out that the functional quality dimension can be perceived in a very subjective manner

### 2.4 *The 'Gap' Model*

The 'Gap' model[5] is a means of describing customer dissatisfaction in the context of service quality. A team from Texas A&M University carried out some interviews with executives in U.S. firms and with consumers. A series of five 'gaps' regarding service quality were then identified:

> "A set of key discrepancies or gaps exists regarding executive perceptions of service quality and the tasks associated with service delivery to consumers. These gaps can be major hurdles in attempting to deliver a service which consumers would perceive as being a high quality."[6]

Five gaps were identified:

(i) Between customers' expectation and managements' perceptions of those expectations, i.e. not knowing what customers expect.

(ii) Between management's perception of customer expectations and service quality specifications, i.e. the wrong service-quality standards.

(iii) Between service quality specifications and service delivery, i.e. the service performance gap.

(iv) Between service delivery and external communications to customers about service delivery, i.e. when promises do not match delivery.

(v) Between customers' expectation and perceived service (the total of the other four gaps).

It is this last 'gap' which has the most significance. The 'Gap' model keeps a clear focus on the perceptions of the customer, and these are seen as paramount.

As part of this research, criteria for evaluating service quality were gathered. Ten key categories were identified which they called 'Service Quality Determinants', and noted that despite the different types of service analysed, consumers used fairly similar criteria. The ten Service Quality Determinants listed by Zeithaml *et al.* were as follows:

(i) *Tangibles:* Appearance of physical facilities, equipment, personnel, and communication materials.

(ii) *Reliability:* Ability to perform the promised service dependably and accurately.

(iii) *Responsiveness:* Willingness to help customers and provide prompt service.

(iv) *Competence:* Possession of the required skills and knowledge to perform the service.

(v) *Courtesy:* Politeness, respect, consideration, and friendliness of contact personnel.

(vi) *Credibility*: Trustworthiness, reliability, honesty of the service provider.

(vii) *Security:* Freedom from danger, risk or doubt.

(viii) *Access:* Approachability and ease of contact.

(ix) *Communication:* Keeping customers informed in language they can understand and listening to them.

(x) *Understanding the customer:* Making efforts to know customers and their needs.

It is possible that these criteria could provide an initial framework for the development of quality criteria in other contexts.

The work on determinants led to the development of a scale for measuring customer perceptions of service quality called SERVQUAL.[8] This scale has been subject to criticism and refinement and there is a continuing debate about the measurement of service quality and the determinants which should be used.

### 3. Total Quality Management

The development of the quality concept in industry has created a requirement for an organisational setup which can prescribe quality concepts at every stage in the planning and delivery of a product or service. The process is called Total Quality Management (TQM). The essence of a TQM strategy is described by Bergman and Klefsjo.[9]

(i) Focus customers

(ii) Base decisions on facts

(iii) Focus on processes

(iv) Improve continuously

(v) Let everybody be committed

The important insight is that quality becomes a continuous process. This is especially important for service industries, where customer perceptions of quality are constantly changing. Quality becomes a process of continuous feedback and improvement.

This process is known as a 'quality system'. Bullivant[10] defines TQM as 'a commitment to a company-wide culture where everyone is clear of the direction and objectives of the organisation and work in support of each other to achieve these goals'. He however, notes that while there is general agreement about the theoretical aspect of TQM, the practical aspects of implementation are more problematic.

## 4. International Standards

National and international standards authorities have turned their attention to quality in recent years. In the UK, the British Standards Institution (BSI) first published BS 5750 in 1979 for quality systems. The latest being the Standards developed by the International Organisation for Standardisation (ISO) into the ISO 9000 series.

A useful definition of quality is found in ISO 8402: 'quality is the totality of features and characteristics of a product or service that bears on its ability to satisfy stated or implied needs.' This has since been refined to 'the totality of characteristics of an entity that bear on its ability to satisfy stated and implied needs'.[11]

The ISO 9000 approach has been applied in many different organisations and obtaining certification can be essential in some industries. Although services can be included in the certification process, ISO 9000 is seen primarily as a product-oriented rather than process-oriented model.

## 5. Benchmarking

Benchmarking is another recent approach to ensuring improvements in quality. Bullivant[12] defines benchmarking as "the continuous process of measuring products, services and practices against leaders, allowing the identification of best practices which will lead to sustained and superior performance". Benchmarking can be carried out with relation to different types of organisation.

(i) *Internal benchmarking:* comparisons with other parts of the same organisation.

(ii) *Competitor benchmarking:* comparisons with a rival organisation.

(iii) *Functional benchmarking:* comparisons with non-competitive organisations carrying out a similar function.

(iv) *Generic benchmarking:* comparison of similar processes in organisations with different functions.

The purpose of the benchmarking process is not just to understand the processes carried out by other organisations, but to enable a considered self-assessment to be made of your own organisation.

**6. Database Quality**

It is only comparatively recent that the library and information community have taken an interest in quality assessment and analysis. In the UK a guide to implementing. BS 5750 and ISO 9000 in libraries was published in 1993[13] and there has been an increasing interest in quality issues in both Germany and the Nordic countries. This interest is largely concerned with issues of quality management of TQM and has led to the development of a set of IFLA guidelines for performance measurement in academic libraries and a draft international standard on library performance indicators. In addition to this emphasis, however, there has been an additional focus on defining information quality both with regard to bibliographic records and with electronic databases. It was the advent of shared computerised cataloguing that made the quality of bibliographic records an issue and studies on this have been carried out both in the UK and USA.

Information quality was not a serious concern for libraries before the advent of electronic databases, Libraries would select books and journals according to their own criteria, which would usually have some reference to users' needs or the requirements of the host organisation. This general approach was later applied to other information formats when they became available, (microforms, video cassettes, LP records, CD-ROMs, etc.) within the financial constraints of the organisation.

Early online databases were regarded with respect by the library users. Basch[14] notes that they were regarded as "nothing short of miraculous" as research tools. For this reason, it was only by the late 1980s that database users began to make suggestions as to how they could be improved. The 1989 Annual Retreat of the Southern California Online Users Group (SCOUG) developed a "user wish list" and the following year, a rating list for database quality.[15]

The rating list was arranged in a set of ten categories:

(i) Consistency

(ii) Coverage and Scope

(iii) Timeliness

(iv) Error rate/Accuracy

(v) Ease of use

(vi) Integration

(vii) Output

(viii) Documentation

(ix) Customer support and Training

(x) Value of cost ratio

**7. The Internet and Information Quality**

SCOUG dedicated their 1995 Annual Retreat to the subject of quality on the Internet. The participants noted that the Internet was quite different to the database industry as most information providers were not motivated primarily by financial considerations. Information providers therefore had little or no incentive to improve the quality of their 'product'. SCOUG also noted that whilst certain technical standards were in place, primarily HTML, and the work being carried out by the WWW Consortium, the Internet Engineering Task Force (IETF) and commercial organisations like Netscape, but there were no content standard. They considered that people might be prepared to pay for a service which gave access to "charted, safe, quality areas" of the Internet. They identified quality issues under the following general headings:

(i) Credibility
(ii) Authority
(iii) Indexing
(iv) Registration
(v) Reviews/Ratings
(vi) Technical
(vii) Security and privacy
(viii) Feedback/Maintenance/Customer service
(ix) Time-size-format, pre-alert warnings
(x) Help files
(xi) Copyright, Intellectual property
(xii) Finding tools
(xiii) Downloading reliability, transparent and standardised
(xiv) Online billing
(xv) Reliable browsable directory of addresses for sites
(xvi) Censorship issues, self-censorship
(xvii) Search engines
(xviii) Advertising
(xix) Payment mechanisms
(xx) Ability to track usage of your site'
(xxi) Maintenance

Because of the nature of the meeting, the quality issues raised by SCOUG do not all refer specifically to information quality but to the Internet generally.

An information Market Observatory report on the quality of eletronic information products and services was published in September 1995.[16] It concentrated on quality issues raised by commercial databases, but did make mention of the Internet. The report identified the main problems as:

(a) Too much information—often redundant and inaccurate,

(b) The lack of centralised control—no editorial function or refereeing.

It also made mention of the World Wide Web (WWW)

"... there is much duplication between sites. Sites and sources can appear, move or disappear very quickly. Websites contain information that ranges from the highly significant through to the trivial and obscene, and because there are no quality controls or any guide to quality, it is difficult for researchers to take information retrieved from the Internet at face value".

It concluded that the Internet "will not become a serious tools for professional searchers until the quality issues are resolved".

Ciolek[17] has argued that if the WWW is to continue to be of use to scholars and the research community quality issues will have to be confronted:

"Our greatest folly seems to be out willingness to cultivate this global communication system, open to all and sundry, without first ensuring that we have enough useful and trustworthy accurate and timely information to be circulated across such a networked behemoth".

Ciolek is the editor of the Information Quality WWW Virtual Library (Ciolek, ed. 1996b) based at the Coombs Computing Unit of the Australian National University in Canberra. This WWW site gives access to information on quality issues and the Internet, and the unit administers a electronic mailing list called Information-Quality-L which acts as a centre for the World-wide exchange of ideas on Internet quality.

**8. Select Parameters for Information Gateways**

An important part of selection process is that certain items are eliminated before the quality evaluation process begins. This includes resources that do not contain any unique information (e.g. only provide links to other resources), resources that have been created by individuals for personal use and those resources which are out-of-date, defunct, inaccurate or superseded.

These evaluation criteria are divided into three main areas:

**8.1 *Information Content***

To what level of detail does the resource go? how superficial/exhaustive is it?

Does the resource contain sufficient basic information, i.e., in a WWW document, contact details, last update details, etc.?

Is the information presented accurately?

Is the information composed well? Is the information within a resource phrased unambiguously?

Is the resource authoritative? who is responsible for the resource? Are they reputable source?

**8.2 *Structural Design and Navigability***

Is the information arranged logically?

Is it easy to navigate the resource?

Are hyperlinks ambiguous, i.e., is it obvious where a link is leading you to?

Are there good back and forward links between pages?

Do you ever find yourself in a position where there are no hyperlinks to anywhere else?

Is the information within a resource arranged consistently?

Is the grammar and spelling accurate?

Are images used effectively or are they over-done?

Is the resource 'viewable' effectively (i.e., without loss of essential information and navigability) in non-graphical browsers?

**8.3** ***Overall Appearance and Usability***

Is the aim and purpose of the resource obvious at first sight?

Is it attractive/functional?

Does it encourage you to explore further?

Is the balance of links and text good?

Is the balance of text, images and white space good?

How big is the resource?

If a WWW document is long, is it navigable? How long does it take to download? Are there single document options for those resources that may be printed?

Are there alternative options for those WWW resources which contain Netscape specific features such as tables?

## 9. Information Gateways and Quality Control: Some Important Considerations

(i) *Accessibility:* The resource has to be accessible. There should be no dead links. Except for some important exceptions, resources should be free to charge. Commercial databases are only included if they contain rare or otherwise unreachable information.

(ii) *Documentation and maintenance* : There should be a minimum of information available about the resource itself—who is providing the information? When was it published, last updated, etc. Editors are supposed to check the resources from time to time, to see whether they are still 'alive'.

(iii) *Reliability of producer organisation* : The editor have to use their subject knowledge for this.

(iv) *Interest* : The resource must be of interest to the technical universities involved, from a research or educational point of view.

(v) *Relevance* : The information should be relevant to the subject area, user profile (i.e. education and research) and within the scope. The information should be substantive—a resource which consists of a collection of links to other resources will normally not be included unless there is substantial annotation or value-added information.

(vi) *Perceived value* : The information should be from an authoritative source. Reputation of information provider, and the information peer reviewed are important considerations

(vii) *Uniqueness* : The resource should not ideally be available else-where (different formats, sites) and

(a) Is there similar/better subject material available?

(b) Does the material have any relation to other works?

(c) Is it an often cited source? Constitute another important points for consideration.

(viii) *Maintenance* : Is the information being maintained/updated? And is the information provider likely to be able to maintain the information? (Unlikely in the case of information provided by students)

(ix) *Presentation of information* : Information should be presented well, easy to use and manage.

## 10. Conclusion

Quality is a diverse concept and has been applied to many things. In management science it is applied to products, services and the process of management itself in TQM. With information, we are mostly concerned with product quality—ensuring that a product, whether it be a journal, electronic database or WWW page, fulfils an agreed set of criteria. Additionally, however, information providers might have some interest in service quality with its emphasis on the expectations and requirements of the customer or user and their fulfilment.

## References

1. Juran, J.M. (1988). The quality function. *In:* Juran, J.M. and Gryna, F.M. (eds.), Juran's quality control handbook, 4th ed. New York: McGra-Hill, pp. 2.1-2.13.
2. Crosby, P.B. (1979). Quality is free: the art of making quality certain, New York: McGraw-Hill.
3. Clark, F.A. (1992). Quality and service: a key focus for performance in the public sector. Working Paper Series HWP 11/92. Henley on Thames: Henley Management College.
4. Gronroos, C (1984). A service quality model and its marketing implications. *European Journal of Marketing*, Vol. 18, no.4, pp. 36-44.
5. Parasuraman, A. Zeithaml, V.A. and Berry L.L. (1985). A conceptual model of service quality and its implications for future research. *Journal of Marketing*, Vol. 49, pp. 41-50.
6. Parasuraman, A. Zeithaml, V.A. and Berry L.L. (1988). SERVQUAL: A multiple-item scale for measuring customer perceptions of service quality. *Journal of Retailing*, Vol. 64, pp. 12-40.
7. Zeithaml, V.A. and Bitner, Mary Jo. Service Marketing. New York: McGraw-Hill, p.36.
8. Parauraman, A, Zeithaml, V.A. and Berry, L.L. (1991). Refinement and reassessment of the SERVQUAL scale. *Journal of Retailing*, Vol. 67, pp. 420-450.
9. Jacso, P (1992). CD-ROM software, dataware and hardware: evaluation, selection and illustration. (Databases searching series, no.4). Englewood, Cole.: Libraries Unlimited.

10. Bullivant, J.R.N. (1994). Benchmarking for continuous improvement in the public sector. Harlow: Longman Information & Reference.
11. ISO 8402: (1994). Quality management and quality assurance—vocabulary. Geneva: International Organisation for Standardization.
12. *Op. cit.*, 10.
13. Norton, R and Ellis, D (1993). Implementing BS 5750. *Aslib Information*, Vol. 21, no. 6; June, pp. 242-245.
14. Basch, T. An overview of quality assurance issues. *In*: Armstrong, C.J. and Hartley, R.J., (eds) Database 2000: UKOLUG state-of-the conference, 1992. Oxford: Learned Information, pp. 85-91.
15. Basch, R (1990a). Databank software for the 1990 and beyond - Part 1, the users' wish list. *Online*, Vol. 14, no. 2, pp. 17-24.
16. Information Market Observatory (IMO) (1995). The quality of electronic information products and services. IMO.
17. Ciolek, T.M. (ed.) (1996b). Information Quality WWW Virtual Library: the Internet guide to construction of quality online resources. <URL: http://coombs.anu.edu.au/WWWVL InfoQuality.html> Accessed: 29 Nov. 1996.

9

# Digital Information Management: Preservation Issues and Strategies

## 1. Introduction

Widespread transition of knowledge from print format to electronic format has also given rise to the problem of its preservation in digital form. The problem of preservation is further complicated by the rapid obsolescence of the hardware and software required to interpret and present digital documents. Ensuring continued access to digital information necessarily involves copying or transforming digital documents to run on current media, software, hardware and operating systems. This paper explores the issues surrounding the preservation of digital information and highlights ways to address them.

## 2. Digital Preservation

"Digital preservation" or "digital archiving" essentially aims at taking steps to ensure the longevity of electronic documents. It applies to documents that are either "born digital" and stored on-line (or on CD-ROM, diskettes or other physical carriers) or to the products of analog-to-digital conversion, if long-term access is intended.

## 3. The Problem

The fundamental problem of preserving electronic

documents or "digital objects" stems from the fact that the the objects unlike non-digital formats are accessible only by using combinations of computer hardware and software. Market competition means that this hardware and software can become obsolete in cycles of less than three years. Ensuring ongoing access, therefore, requires currency with technology changes, and moving digital objects from obsolete to current file formats, storage media, operating systems and so on.

A number of other technical, social and legal issues add to the difficulty of the task. These include

- the increasing complexity of digital objects (incorporating text, images, audio, video in various formats) and their increasing software dependence (e.g., storage in databases);
- the rapidly increasing number of digital objects and proliferation of document standards and formats;
- the lack of planning to incorporate preservation needs in systems and lack of availability of off-the-shelf products supporting preservation needs;
- the lack of consideration of long-term access requirements when creating digital products;
- the absence of widely-accepted standards which will assure access over time;
- copyright/intellectual property rights that may interfere with the ability to preserve digital objects through systematic copying;
- unstable storage media (e.g., diskettes) whose life span is limited;
- a lack of technical expertise in collections managers and preservation experts;

**4. Preservation Requirements**

Preservation measures ensure that a document digital or otherwise is accessible in a usable form over time.

Maintaining the accessibility of digital media, however, is much more complex than with such non-digital media as paper. For example, when a book is preserved in its original format, *all* aspects of the book are preserved. It is practically impossible to extract individual elements (e.g., content without layout) because they are inextricably linked. Even reformatting to paper or microfilm does not completely divorce content from layout as page sequences and physical appearance, for instance, can still be captured. Digital objects, in contrast, are easily decomposed into individual elements, and significantly more effort must be made to preserve them as a "whole." For example, one can retain the content of an electronic document, while losing the layout. Further, one can keep its physical presence (i.e., a file), but fail to preserve its readability.

In the digital world, then, the first task is to identify the multiple aspects of a work that must be preserved. Next, to succeed in the preservation of digital objects, preservation measures must ensure that as many of these aspects as possible persist over time. In preserving a digital object, we aim to:

### 4.1 *Integrity of Object*

A book is a book, or it exists in a set, but what are the boundaries of a document in a hypertext environment? The boundaries of digital objects are less clear, especially if they are compound objects created by assembling different media or by linking to resources from around a network.

### 4.2 *Physical Preservation*

The physical presence in this case refers to the computer file, the series of "1"s and "0"s that are the basis of a digital object.

### 4.3 *Content Preservation*

This aspect refers to maintaining the ability to access the content at its lowest level, such as ASCII text, without the embellishments of font variations and layout features.

### 4.4 *Presentation Format*

Content is typically rendered in some presentation, format or layout, that includes different font faces and sizes, the use of white space, columns, marginalia, headers, footers, pagination, and so on. In many types of digital documents (e.g., SGML, XML, and some forms of PDF), the layout specifications are separate from the content. To retain the original look of a document, these layout specifications must also be preserved, especially when they contribute significantly to the understanding and interpretation of the content.

### 4.5 *Functionality*

Digital objects have a functionality that goes far beyond traditional paper documents. They can contain multimedia components (i.e., text, graphics, audio, and video), exist in hypertext format.

### 4.6 *Authenticity*

An individual accessing the object must be able to verify that it is the one s/he wants, and that the transformations to keep it accessible have preserved its original form. Thus, activities to guard authenticity include securing digital objects against unauthorized changes and monitoring digital objects through multiple "copying" cycles to ensure that each copy is an acceptable reedition of the original Establishing authoritative depositories would also help achieve this goal.

### 4.7 *Location and Reference*

Digital objects can be readily altered, copied or moved. An individual must be able to match a citation to a digital object, and to distinguish it from other versions or editions.

### 4.8 *Provenance*

Provenance is an archival concept that asserts the origin and chain of custody of an object and contributes to defining it as a whole. Imprint statements and bookplates, for example, partly fill this role for formally published items. Establishing an object's origin and history help confirm that the work is authentic and its content is intact.

### 4.9 *Preserve context*

Digital objects are partly defined by their hardware and software dependencies, their mode of distribution and linkages to other digital objects. Preserving digital objects may mean weaning them from some technical dependencies, changing the mode of distribution, and deactivating links. In these circumstances, preserving context is a particular challenge.[1]

## 5. Preservation Strategies

Several strategies attempt to address the primary digital preservation problem of technological obsolescence. These include migrating information through successive generations of technology; using software to emulate the behavior of older machines; preserving original hardware and software to run obsolete programs, and creating hard copies (paper or microform) of digital objects. Each of these strategies meets some, but not all, preservation goals.

### 5.1 *Migration and Transfer*

Migration is the primary strategy articulated by most organizations that plan to preserve digital objects. It covers a range of activities to periodically copy, convert or transfer digital information from one generation of technology to subsequent ones. Migration may involve copying digital information from a medium that is becoming obsolete or physically deteriorating to a newer one (e.g., floppy disk to CD-ROM), and/or converting from one format to another (e.g., Microsoft Word to ASCII), and/or moving documents from one platform to another (e.g., VAX to UNIX). Migration certainly preserves the physical presence and the content of a digital object. However, it may not preserve presentation, functionality and context. For example, presentation elements such as bolding and italics may disappear, and the functionality and context provided by links between database entries may be lost because the links break. Successive migrations may eventually result in unacceptable data loss.[2] The focus is on limiting the loss and retaining the content in a usable form. Migration is undeniably an important strategy for preserving digital objects. However, it has yet to be tested and proven as a mechanism for managing complex multimedia objects over the long term.

### 5.2 *Emulation*

Emulation refers to creating new software that mimics the operations of older hardware or software in order to reproduce its performance. Thus, not only are physical presence and content preserved, but digital objects could display original features (e.g., layout) and functionality available with the older software. Emulation has recently attracted attention as a potential strategy to assist preservation, recognizing that some electronic material that is highly dependent on particular hardware and software will not lend itself to migration.

Emulation is used to provide "backward compatibility" for video games, and to model how future systems might run. Emulators exist for some obsolete systems, however, emulation for preserving digital objects over the long term has not been widely tested or priced.

### 5.3 *Output to Paper or Microfilm*

Outputting a hard copy of a digital file is a "low tech" solution that can result in a well-standardized product with a life expectancy of several hundred years. Certainly, this strategy could fix the object as a whole and preserve content and to some extent layout. However, a decreasing number of publications (flat files, printable formats) lend themselves to such methods. For example, output to paper will lead to great functional loss for hypertext documents, and cannot capture multimedia. Despite these drawbacks, a "hybrid strategy" of creating both microfilm and digital copies is gaining support as a technique for reformatting paper originals. The digital copy enhances access and functionality, and the microform copy acts as an archival surrogate.

### 5.4 *Preservation Technology*

Another method for ensuring ongoing access to digital objects would be to simply keep older technology available for use. Although this would preserve content and enable future generations to view digital objects in their native format with original layout and functionality, creating hardware or software "museums" is prohibitive in cost, space and technical support requirements. At best, this method is an interim measure when migration is not possible.

## 6. Control

To increase the probability that digital objects will be preserved, organizations need to lay appropriate groundwork. One way is to develop and implement the most effective practices in acquiring, describing and managing digital resources.

### 6.1 *Standards*

To facilitate preservation, the best practice is to adopt a three-part approach:

1) use current standards to create digital objects;
2) monitor standards as they change;
3) migrate to new standards as they are established.

Most digital preservation guidelines advocate collecting digital objects in standard formats. Unfortunately, while standards are well defined for text (e.g., ASCII), images (e.g., JPEG, TIFF) and encoding documents (e.g., SGML, HTML), standards have not emerged for some other types of information (e.g., databases). In addition, not only do standards change rapidly, but vendors seeking to increase their market share incorporate "value-added" features to accepted standards. Institutions performing the digital preservation activity can also be subject to standardization.

The International Standards Organization (ISO) has produced a reference model (CCSDS 650.0-W-4.0), for an Open Archival Information System (OAIS).[3] The model establishes the minimum requirements for a digital archive to ensure long-term preservation of digital information, and provides a framework for describing and comparing archival architecture and operation.

## 7. Developing Digital Preservation Guidelines

Archives and record-keeping bodies in Europe, North America and Australia have taken the lead in developing best practices and functional requirements that address some preservation issues.[4] Common elements include

- Recognizing the creator's responsibility to preserve his/her work initially;
- Identifying responsibilities of the archive;
- Adopting appropriate selection guidelines (which emphasize standards when a choice of formats exists);
- Securing archived items from intentional or unintentional alteration;
- Providing contextual documentation including a history of creation, transmission and use, and audit trails;
- Describing digital objects completely.

Some libraries have developed similar guidelines. However, a recent survey concluded that most digital preservation guidelines focus on creation, receipt and capture of digital objects, and do not satisfactorily address their long-term preservation.[5]

### 7.1 *Documenting Resources*

A recurrent theme in digital preservation guidelines is documentation and description of electronic resources. The need for such deliberate description stems in part from the fact that digital objects do not carry the visible evidence of creation and use (imprints, bindings, bookplates, marginalia, or Scotch tape) of non-electronic formats. Such clues guide preservation decisions. They also help users to establish that the work is whole and intact, and to understand its provenance and the context in which it was created.

### 7.2 *Metadata*

A description of a digital object is "data about data," or metadata. Such descriptive data should include the contextual information crucial to the long-term management of electronic information. Metadata elements useful in preservation might include

- Identifiers ;
- Hardware, operating system and software required to access a document;
- Physical details of tangible format publications such as CD-ROM, floppy disks;
- encoding standard and version;
- migration history and its success;
- data to assist determining authenticity;
- rights management information;
- versions and dates.

Conversion projects would employ additional metadata elements such as the capture device, resolution, compression, source material, and producer (of the digital document). Existing metadata schemes (e.g., MARC, Dublin Core) provide for some such information capture, but there is no consensus on which approach will work best for preservation purposes. In MARC, for example, some of the necessary data is captured in notes' fields that may not use sufficiently detailed or consistent language for subsequent search and retrieval.

### 7.3 *Unique identifiers*

One element of describing a digital object is to assign it a unique and persistent identifier. An identifier is a number, like an ISBN, which is associated with a particular instance of a digital object. Unlike an URL, it is independent of the location of that object. A unique, widely supported identifier for digital objects would help establish the authenticity of the object by confirming to a user that the resource s/he is accessing the one cited. It could also help establish the relationship between copies or versions of digital objects, as any modification of the original would result in a modification of its identifier. Some organizations involved in digital preservation are currently using PURLs (Persistent Uniform Resource Locators),URNs (Uniform Resource Names) or modified Digital Object Identifiers. As yet, no single digital identifier has achieved widespread, international acceptance.

### 7.4 *Linking Metadata with Content*

Metadata can be stored either as an integral part of the document it describes (e.g., embedded in an HTML header) or as part of a separate file of information (e.g., a MARC record). One way of linking metadata and the digital object is to package them together. To this end, the aforementioned Reference Model for an Open Archival Information System (OAIS) proposes an "information package" comprised of "content information" and "preservation descriptive information"[6]. Along similar lines, a working group of the Society of Motion Picture and Television Engineers has developed a Universal Preservation Format (UPF),[7] a data-file mechanism that uses a container structure to incorporate metadata into digital media objects. Although primarily developed for audio-visual data, the principles underlying the UPF may have wider applicability.

### 7.5 *Establishing Infrastructure*

A final way in which libraries are gaining control over the preservation of digital objects is by building preservation requirements into systems development. The Australian National Library, for example, has started a Digital Services Project to develop systems to manage its digital collections and to support cooperative, shared access.[8]

The next steps remain ill defined. To reduce the uncertainty surrounding digital preservation, we can encourage creators to use practices that will aid long-term preservation, such as creating valid documents in standard document formats and address the question of which preservation strategy will work best by testing migration and emulation and identifying associated costs and tradeoffs in each case.

**8. Conclusion**

Rapid technological obsolescence combined with relatively short-lived media means that collections must be actively managed. Simply collecting and "shelving" important works, a passive strategy that works to some extent for paper-based publications, is insufficient to ensure digital objects will survive in perpetuity.

**References**

1. Preserving digital information: report of the Task Force on Archiving of Digital Information commissioned by the Commission on Preservation and Access and the Research Libraries Group. Washington, D.C.: Commission on Preservation and Access, 1996. <http://www.rlg.org/ArchTF/>
2. Colin Webb, "Migration Trials: Migrating publications on floppy disk to CD-R". October 1997. <http://www.nla.gov.au/nla/staffpaper/cwebb7.html> (Jan. 20, 1999)
3 <http://www.leeds.ac.uk/cedars/>
4. <http://www.news.cornell.edu/releases/Nov98/preserving.digital.bs.html>
5. The full text of this report, titled "Avoiding Technological Quicksand: Finding a Viable Technological Foundation for Digital Preservation", is available at <http://www.clir.org/pubs/reports/reports.html>

6. Consultative Committee for Space Data Systems. 1998. Reference Model for an Open Archival Information System (OAIS), ed. L. Reich and D. Sawyer. CCSDS 650.0-W-3.0. White Book, 17 September, 1998, p. 17
7. UPF Homepage: <http://info.wgbh.org/upf/>
8. The National Library of Canada has incorporated preservation requirements in its Digital Library Infrastructure Project. The next step is to develop the systems.

# 10

# Accessing Information: A Framework for Policy Making

## 1. Introduction

Information is a basic resource for all human beings, and it is as important to us as food, air, and rest. It is the basis for all our decisions. Information is needed for personal decisions as minor as when to go to bed to as significant as buying a house. Information is also the basis for running the organizations in which we work. Policies concerning information, both governmental and private, have the potential to have a profound effect on society.

It is 'intelligence' information which enables government to make decisions concerning foreign policy: it is social information which allows it to make decisions concerning education programs: and it is information about all aspects of health care that is consuming Health experts. Governmental policies can provide wide access to information or restrict access. All public policy is made on the basis of information available at the time of the decision. Therefore, information policy provides the basis, or the support, for all other public policy. The availability of information has made the crucial difference in many public policy decisions. Policies about the collection, storage, use and dissemination of information form the basis of information policy. It is this attribute, the all encompassing nature of information, that makes it so difficult and complex. The formulation of information policy is one of the most important aspects of public policy.

## 2. Need for a Policy

Change in the information environment is the basis for communication, both personal and scholarly. Therefore, policies governing access to information can have dramatic effects on the scholarly communication process. For example, governmental policies concerning classifed information have partially determined what topics military historians can choose to explore. In substance access to information determines many choices that scholars make concerning what to study. If access is not provided, study cannot proceed. As we move to the use of information through electronic media we find that relationships between information, the producer, and the consumer are changing. Spender[1] proposes that each information medium has its own social structure. As communication has moved from verbal to print and to electronic the relationships between writer and reader and between lay citizen and scholar have changed. Those who were the repositories of information were the authorities. They preserved the knowledge base for society and chose to whom knowledge was to be communicated. These authorities were the authors and users of information, so they held great power in society. When writing and printing came into common use, this power relationship changed. Through the printed page, information could be exchanged without direct contact between people. Paper proved to be both durable and transportable. Printing allowed education to become widespread. However, authoring essentially remained with scholars and professionals. Printing was, and still is, an expensive investment. Access was primarily given to those with appropriate education and credentials—givin them the authority to communicate information. With the advent of information, in electronic form the relationship between the author and the user of information is changing further. Electronic information can, and does, move anywhere at anytime. A mere change in the way information is stored, from paper to electronic, has produced a significant change and geography is no longer important. The place where a piece of information is stored has become less relevant as information earlier used to be stored on paper, these pieces of paper can only be at one place at one time—essentially controlling access to that information. Physical access was required for intellectual access; in order to read it physically in your hand. Today, information stored in electronic form can be easily accessed from thousands of miles away. Exact copies can be made without the owner of the original losing his or her copy or even knowing that it has been shared with anothe person.

Access to information has vastly increased for those who know how to gain this access. The ability to control access to information, for any reason, is challenged in a war without precedent in our history. This ease of access has changed the relationship between author and user. It is much more difficult for the author to restrict access. Control shifting from the author to the user. In addition, it is also easier to become an author. Many electronic networks provide free access to information, both as a user and also as an author, making it easy for authors to add their thoughts to the knowledge base. The increased availability of information in electronic formats has substantially decreased control over information as a whole.

The evolution of public policy, however, has not kept pace with this vast technological change. Setting public policy in this area poses a daunting challenge even for information professionals. There currently exist a vast number of laws, regulations, directives, statements, policies and judicial interpretations concerning information. Given

this complexity, how does an information professional balance all the compeing needs? How can we organize our thinking about information policy?

## 3. A Framework for Information Policy

Given the complexity of information policy, a system to organize our thinking would be a valuable asset. Overman and Cahill[2] have provided a framework which can be used to study information policy issues. This paper will cover three of the information policy values defined by Overman and Cahill. These three values are (i) access—the ability to gain access to records held by governments or private companies; (ii) privacy—as individual's right to hold information about him/herself secure; and (iii) intellectual property—the ownership of information. These three values comprise the major components for the current information policy debate.

### 3.1 *Access*

There is nothing more basic to the relationship between government and citizens than the right of access to information. The free flow of information is essential to the citizenry's ability to participate in democratic government.[3] It has been generally agreed that information access is a citizen's entitlement, particularly in this information age[4]. As a public policy concept, access has been widely accepted.

Librarians stand at the focal point for support of the free flow of information; access is of a fundamental value for the profession. However, there are other information policy considerations which must be balanced with open and free access. One of those considerations is needed for government to function effectively. Experience has taught us that openess within a democratic system does not always bring effective decision making. Therefore, most access laws limit disclosure by providing for exceptions to open records and meetings. At both levels of government, information can be withheld for reasons of effective government.

### 3.2 *Privacy*

Privacy, the right of an individual to hold personal information private, is also thought to be grounded in democratic governance. Privacy can be defined as an integral part of freedom; an important aspect of the ability to secure autonomy. This "right" is strongly supported within Indian Constitution.[5] Privacy has become an increasingly important concept in the information policy area. As access values have been implemented into law, the concern for privacy has grown. In the USA at the federal level, there is strong court-interpreted support for a "right of privacy". In United States the most comprehensive privacy legislation at the federal level is the Privacy Act of 1974. There is also federal legislation dealing with specific types of records, such as financial records in banks and other financial institutions. At the state level, there is stronger legislative support of privacy. Eleven States have a constitutional provision guaranteeing privacy, and six states have a statutory law protecting privacy[6]. Privacy is also recognized in open meeting and open records legislation.

The information policy values of access and privacy are both important to democratic governance. The balance struck between these values is one of the most difficult aspects of current information policy. The transition to electronic information has made policy making in this area even more important. As noted earlier, electronic information is more difficult to control. This tilt of legislation at both the federal and state level has been in favour of access, leaving privacy issues more often to interpretation[7] by courts. The lack of strong legislative guarantees, combined with the difficulty of enforcement has created an information policy environment where privacy is far from guaranteed.[8] Threats to privacy have become a concern for the general public. In a recent poll in the United States, more than two-thirds of the public agreed that computers are a threat to personal privacy. Widespread privacy violations have been reported on a consistent basis, most recently in a well documented book by Jeffrey Rathfeder[9]. He concludes that the electronic information kept by government and private business are readily available. If privacy is to be guaranteed, it is clear that information policy must change. Part of that change must be clearer definition of who owns and controls pieces of information.

### 3.3 *Intellectual Property*

Ownership of information, or intellectual property, is an increasingly important aspect of information policy. The government has a substantial interest in protecting free expression by guaranteeing that citizens can use ideas for their own benefit and the benefit of others. At the same time government has an interest in guaranteeing the people's welfare by encouraging intellectual advancement that benefits society. In a capitalistic economy, this advancement is accomplished by allowing the ownership of expression. Limiting access to information by providing for ownership fulfils this public policy need.

Most intellectual property laws in the USA exist at the federal level. Copyright law protects the expression of ideas in any form, such as literary, musical, dramatic, graphic, and ornamental works; however, ideas that have not yet found expression are excluded. In essence, the idea itself is not protected, but the expression of the idea is. Inventions which perform some useful function are protected through federal patent law. Abstract ideas are not patentable; a patent requires actual application. Trade secret law, which exists at the state level, is the third component of intellectual property law. These laws protect information that has independent economic value from generally known and from benefiting anyone other than the originator.

All three components of intellectual property law combine to comprise a fairly strong system of protection. However, electronic information poses a significant challenge to the current law. Software programs fall in between copyright and patent protection. They are expressions of ideas, and yet hold great utility. Legislators have not yet been able to revise current law to adequately protect such intellectual property. The courts have had a difficult time sorting out the issues of ownership given the inadequate laws. This situation has left software producers in a difficult position. With the rapid change in technology, this type of intellectual property tends to have a short life span. Many software producers are moving towards trade secret law to ensure protection of their electronic intellectual property, which appears to afford them better protection in the short term.

### 4. Conclusion

This brief presentation provides a basic framework for issues concerning information policy. These issues are critical to the future of the information professionals as well as to the daily functioning of all citizens. The choices we make affect governance, personal privacy, and the scholarly communication process. Given the complexity of these issues, it is difficult to see how one might choose between the options.

Given the complexity of information policy, a beginning might be made by having statement of basic principles. There are three statements of principles that are useful tools in deciding information policy issues.

The most comprehensive set of principles dealing with personal information was issued by the Organization for

Economic Co-operation and Development (OECD)[10]. These principles provide limits on the collection personal data as wall as its use. They also discuss the rights of an individual to challenge the accuracy of collected data. While these principles have been used as a model in the USA for the federal privacy act and legislation at the state level, the government is far from guaranteeing privacy as proposed by these principles. The National Commission on Libraries and Information Science there has approved a set of principles which reaffirms that the information policies of the US government are based on the freedom guaranteed by the Constitution, and on the recognition of public information as a national resource to be developed and preserved in the public interest[11]. These principles discuss access rights, privacy issues, accuracy of information, and cost issues. These principles are an excellent beginning towards forming a more comprehensive set of access. EDUCOM has issued a Bill of Rights which defines information policy principles specifically related to electronic information[12]. These principles cover individual and institutional rights and reponsibilities dealing with access, privacy, and ownership issues. Also included are freedom of speech issues and issues surrounding learning to use electronic resources. Cost factors are also included as an issue for institutions to consider. These principles provide a basis on which an individual institution or library could write an information policy.

Ultimately, it is responsible government and responsible citizens who must decide the right use of information and the right balance between access, privacy, and ownership. The determination of information policy will affect all information and professionals in coming years. The decisions made are likely to affect the most democratic of these institutions—the library. It is vitally important for information professionals to become well informed and active in the formation of information policy.

## References

1. Spewder (Dale). 'Electronic scholarship: Perform or perish?'. *In* Woman, Information Technology, and Scholarship, ed by H. Jeanie Taylor, Cheris Ksamarae, and Maureen Ebben 1993. University of Illinois, Urbana, Ill. pp. 15-19.
2. Overman (E. Samue) and Cahill (Anthony G.). Information policy: A study of values in the policy process. *Policy Studies Review* 9, 4 1990.
3. Madison (James). "Letter to U.T. Barry, 4 August 1822:" *In* the writings of James Madison, ed by Gaillard Hunt, 1910, Putnam, New York, pp. 142-44.
4. Gavison (Ruth). "Privacy and the limits of the law." *In* Philosophical dimensions of privacy: An anthology, ed. by Ferdinand David Schoeman, 1984. Cambridge University Press. New York, pp. 346-402.
5. Godyear (Mary Lou). Information and democracy: A study of the relationship between state information policies and democratic governance.
6. *Ibid*.
7. Kidd (Rita). Public information gatekeepers. *Government Technology*, 6, 4; 1993 ; 20.
8. Thomas (Rosita). Privacy in the age of computer. *CRS Review*, 11, 1; 1990; 8.
9. Rothfeder (Jeffrey). Privacy for sale: How computerization has made everyone's private life an open secret, New York, Simon and Schuster, 1992.
10. Organization for Economic Co-operation and Development. Guidelines on the protection of privacy and transborder flows of personal data. 1981 OECD, Paris.
11. National Commission on Library Information Science. Principles of public information. *In* Citizen rights and access to electronic information, ed by Dennis J. Reynolds. 1992. Library and Information Technology Association, Chicago, p. 175.
12. Connolly (Frank) and Webster (Sally). Bill of Rights and Responsibilities for electronic learner. *EDUCOM Review*. 28, 3; 1993: 24-7.

# 11

# Information Technology and Public Policy: A Socio-Human Profile of Indian Digital Revolution

## 1. Introduction

Information technology has emerged as the most potent tool to collect, organise and disseminate information to the people at large scale through communication networks. It is one of the fastest spreading technologies in the world in terms of use and production. It is diffusing rapidly into all industrial and service sectors and is seen as one of the most crucial technologies affecting economic growth in developing countries. Its use is ubiquitous in the industrialized countries to the extent that in United States investment in IT accounts for about 50% of total new capital investment by corporations. The production of IT products and services is a major industry in the US, Japan and Europe. Several newly industrialized countries, such as China, Korea, Taiwan, Singapore and Brazil have become significant producers and users of IT.

This evolution of IT has been marked by heavy government involvement in virtually all countries.

Of all the newly industrializing countries, India stands out for the degree to which its governments has intervened in the IT sector and the complexity and nuance of that intervention.

This paper discusses various aspects of India's Information Technology policies and focuses on the relationship among policies and outcome in terms of its impact on prevailing socio-economic conditions of the people.

## 2. Information Technology : Infrastructure

The assimilation of any new technology requires the presence of an infrastructure with which to acquire, learn and successfully apply the technology. This includes sufficiently available human resources, well developed telecommunication networks, research and development capabilities and capital for investments.

### 2.1 *Human Resources*

India, a country of more than 1 billion people, turns out an estimated 400,000 graduates with technical and engineering degrees per year constituting the third largest pool of engineering and scientific manpower in the world and second largest pool of English speaking manpower with IT qualifications. According to a recent survey of National Association of Software and Services Companies (NASSCOM) from a base of 6,800 IT software and services professionals knowledge workers in 1985-86, the number is projected to increase to 522,000 shortly. But the NASSCOM projections also reveal a shortage of nearly 530,000 of IT professionals over the next 3 years, assuming optimistic growth in industry. **(NASSCOM, 2002)**

### 2.2 *Telecommunications*

A good telecommunications network is another vital element of IT infrastructure. Since 1985 the government has initiated a new telecommunication policy to strengthen the telecommunications sector and from 7$^{th}$ five year plan onwards, the sector is identified as one of the top development priorities. **(India, Planning Commission, 2002)** The telecommunication sector has now been widely opened to private players and is attracting massive investment. The government is progressively moving from a structure where the incumbent operator was a part of the government to a structure where the incumbent operator is corporatized and subsequently privatized.

### 2.3 *Research and Development*

India's R&D expenditures are well ahead of other developing countries in the Asia-Pacific region but the business R & D accounts for only 13% of the total and R&D is largely conducted by public sector and universities where it is not that relevant to economic application. In an effort to remove this anomaly, the government is establishing "science cities" around research institutions to serve as centers for high tech industrial development.

### 2.4 *Capital*

Initially capital for investment in information technology was scarce thus making the broad environment for IT diffusion very poor. However situation began to change drastically under the policy of economic restructuring and reforms initiated in the year 1991.

## 3. IT Policy : Historical Overview

The history of IT Policy in Indian can be divided into two distinct periods. From the mid-1960s through the early 1980s policies aimed at achieving technological self-sufficiency through state production, regulation of private production. The second period, from 1984 to early 1990s, saw a shift in focus to moderate liberalization of the industry and promotion of domestic IT production.

Another era is now in the making as the government moves towards more extensive liberalization of the economy.

### 3.1 *1960s and 1970s : Indigenization and self sufficiency*

India was motivated to try to develop self sufficiency in computers and electronics largely by national security concerns related to border conflicts with China and Pakistan. The government created an Electronics Committee to devise a strategy for achieving self sufficiency in Electronics. The main vehicle chosen to gain access to advanced computer technology was negotiation with multinationals, primarily IBM, which accounted for 70% of all computers installed in India from 1960-1972.

In an attempt of satisfy the government's interest in developing domestic production, both IBM and British owned ICL (International Computers Limited) began to refurbish the used computes in Indian plants and sell them to Indian customers. IBM felt that Indian should evolve technologically from one level of sophistication to the next.

A 1966 report by the Electronics Committee objected to step-by-step technological evolution and recommended that India should leap ahead to the latest technologies. Government however failed to impose its will on IBM due to its strong position with users and export earnings. The government's early attempts to regulate the IT sector worsened the degree of technological backwardness.

In 1966 the responsibility for implementing the Electronics Committee report strategies was given to Department of Defense Supplies, with monitoring by a new agency, the Electronic Committee of India. In 1971 the government announced the formation of Department of Electronics (DoE) and a new Electronics Commission, responsible for policy formulation and oversight for day-to-day implementation of policies. In 1975 the DoE was given power over the licensing of computer imports and the first step taken by it was the establishment of Santa Cruz Electronics Export Processing Zone (SEEPZ) near Bombay followed by the creation of state-owned ECIL

(Electronics Corporation of India Ltd.) as a national champion in mini computer production.

In 1975, in a landmark development, the US computer maker. Burroughs, entered into a joint venture with Tata Consultancy Services to export software and printers from SEEPZ. In the same year governments established Computer Maintenance Corporation (CMC) with a legal monopoly on the maintenance of all foreign computer systems in the country, reducing the advantage which IBM had with the users.

In 1978, due to increasing political pressure IBM quit India which was a seminal event. Illustrating the extent of government's ability to exert its power over Multinational Corporations and direct the IT development in India. One effect of IBM's departure was to open the market to a number of competitors, including ECIL, ICL and Tata Borroughs.

### 3.2 *1980s :Partial Liberalization and Industry Promotion*

India's IT policies in 1980s were aimed at modernizing a industry that was estimated to be about 15 years behind the current frontiers of research and production. In a departure from the import substitution approach of the past, exports software and peripherals were now promoted and the import of mainframes and supercomputers were encouraged under certain conditions.

### 3.3 *The New Computer Policy of 1984*

The new computer policy of 1984 announced by DoE **(India, Department of Electronics, 1984)** aimed at promoting the manufacturing of computers based on latest technology, at prices comparable to international levels and with progressively increased indigenization. An Important policy change was the liberalization of imports to foster domestic hardware. Duty levels were lowered on components needed by computer manufacturers and companies producing CPUs, peripherals and subsystems were permitted liberal imports of "Know-how" with a low excise duty.

### 3.4 *1986 : Software Policy*

Following up on the 1984 hardware policy, the Department of Electronics (DoE) announced the 1986 policy on Computer Software Export, Software Development and Training. **(India, Department of Electronics, 1986)** The main objectives of the policy were to promote the integrated development of software in the country for domestic as well as export markets and to promote the use of computers as a tool to decision making and to promote appropriate applications that will catalyze economic development software imports and the duty was reduced to 60% which was further reduced in 1992 to 25% for computes and software used software producers.

In 1990, a 100% income tax exemption was extended to profits from software exports and the double taxation of software imports was eliminated. It was also decided to develop twelve additional software technology parks.

Though India's IT Policies have focussed heavily on regulations of foreign as well domestic producers and on protection of domestic market and the 1984 and 1986 policies consisted mostly of loosening of existing regulations, still a number of programmers, initiatives and institutions have been established to implement policy and promote various aspects of IT.

The DoE invests in IT and R&D through large multiyear programs involving various research units. The Knowledge-Based Computer Systems (KBCS) programme involves the five IITs, The Indian Institute of Science in Bangalore and the National Centre for Software Technology (NCST) in Bombay. The Education and Research in Computer Networking (ERNET) experiments with new concepts in computer networking and promotes Integrated Services Digital Network (ISDN).

In 1988, the National Informatics Center set up NICNET, a satellite-based computer communication network connecting 439 cities and towns to support computerization of governments at the central, state and districts level. A Computer Aided Design project was set up with links to five centers, and a Computer Aided Management Infrastructure has been established with feeder centers in four cities. A number of projects have been undertaken to promote IT use in public and private sectors and to mobilize a favorable bias towards its use.

Government's attempts to spur the development of an indigenous IT industry have been quite successful and after the 1984 Computer Policy announcement production shot up by 100% while prices declined by 50%. A boom in minicomputer sales began when HCL dropped its prices dramatically, starting in price war that greatly increased the affordability of PCs.

### 3.5 *1991 to 1996: Impact of Economic Liberalization*

During this period, the IT policy was affected by general changes in industrial policy. Early in 1991 its import became more difficult thanks to the devaluation of the rupee, raising the software import duty to 112 per cent. Simultaneously there was an effort to encourage exports by streamlining the process for exports incentive payments and for creation of export-only units. There were several software related promotional measures during this period, including reduction in telecommunication charges for satellite links, duty-free import of telecommunication equipment into EPS, excise duty exemptions.

At the end of 1992, the DoE was reorganized to emphasize its promotional rather than regulatory role. It amended and updated interventions in areas such as training and research and development. The Copyright Act was also amended, confirming that raids, fines and prison sentence could be used against software pirates. Import rules were also changed and liberalization gathered pace for software.

Duty for software import was reduced to 110 per cent in 1992, 85 per cent in 1993, split in 1994 to 20 per cent for applications software and 65 per cent for system software and then reduced to 10 per cent for both categories 1995. **(Export & Import Policy, 1995)** In April 1993, duplication of software in India was permitted for the first time.

The beginning of 1990s also witnessed emergence of Software Technology Parks of India (STPI) under the state initiative. STPI was created as autonomous organization under the Department of Electronics, to provide facilities such as duty-free import of capital goods, income tax holiday for 10 years, high-speed data communication links etc.

The year 1996 can be described as landmark year in the history of information technology as Internet service was started in India by Videsh Sanchar Nigam Limited, a public sector company with a great promise. The policy makers recognized the potential of the Net for a quantum group in the knowledge-based economy. The subsequent ISP policies of the Department of Telecommunications (DOT) were very pragmatic with free licensing to ISPs. Setting up of gateways for Internet, laying of fibers and cables was freely permitted to the ISPs. Tax incentives were showered on the industry, infrastructure status given and mergers and acquisitions facilitated.

India was one of the few countries to enact the Information Technology Act in year 2000 to enable digital signatures. It aims to provide the legal infrastructure for e-commerce in India. **(India, Ministry of Communication and Information Technology, 2002)**

## 4. IT : Proliferation and Application

### 4.1 *Economics*

In a very short time, India has risen to considerable eminence in the world of information technology, enlarging from $ 1.73 billion in 1994-95 to a $ 13.5 billion industry in 2001-02. In terms of share of GDP, the IT industry figures have risen from 0.59 per cent to 2.87 per cent in 2001-02. According to the NASSCOM report revenues from hardware, peripherals and networking are estimated to touch $ 2,983 millions during 2001-02, India's software and services exports are expected to account for $ 7,678 millions of revenues. Revenue from IT enabled services sector grew from US$ 554 million in 1999-2000 to US$ 897 million in 2000-2001 Customer Interaction Services, which included call centers and customer support centers were the prime areas of growth. In 1999-2000, the volume of e-commerce transactions in India was only US$ 104 million whereas this is a growing segment in the international market. **(NASSCOM, 2002)**

The Indian domestic IT market has been spurred by various developments including a growth in PC penetration, increased usage of networking and peripheral equipment and proliferation of software application.The Internet revolution is sweeping across the country, coupled with lowering hardware prices and cheaper bandwidth availability. Within eight years, predicts a recent study by McKinsey & Co. and the NASSCOM, India's annual IT exports could hit $50 billion — about 33 per cent of global software exports. Such a surge is expected to generate 2.2 million jobs — and push our growth rate near the double digits that many East Asian Tigers enjoyed before the 1997 crash.

### 4.2 *Governance*

In a recent policy initiative the government has recommended each ministry to allocate 2-3 per cent of its budget on IT promotion. Central Government has taken various steps, legislative, regulatory and promotional measures to facilitate IT use in corporate, financing and taxation matters. Different projects have been initiated to come up with IT based solutions for development purposes. Different ministries and departments have come out with their web sites. Major areas of computerization include railway reservation, allocation of Permanent Account Number (PAN) for Income Tax payers, processing of passport, results of public examination, Regional Transport Offices, custom clearance, schemes under implementation by the NGOs, vigilance information, single counter services and VSAT based money order under the Department of Post, computerization of Supreme Court cases, land records, Parliament questions, debates and deliberations.

Central and State government and their field organizations, financial institutions, insurance companies, educational institutions are proceeding ahead with introduction of computerization and use of IT in the sphere of work. It is reported that 12,000 out of 45,000 bank branches have implemented major computerization.

Many state governments have declared IT policies. State effort to promote IT is through development of IT infrastructure, e-governance, IT education and providing enabling environment for IT proliferation. Substantial growth in demand for Internet and PCs has been experienced in the recent past. There are 1.6 million estimated Internet connections in India in August 2000 as against 0.14 million in March 1998. The number of Internet subscribers in the year 2004-05 are likely to reach 7.7 million, with the user base increasing to 50 millions. The PC base in India, according to a survey of the NASSCOM, numbered 5 million, i.e., 5 per 1000 people in August 2001 as against 3 per 1000 in 1999. The NASSCOM forecasts PC prices to decline to by nearly 40 per cent and PC penetration to reach 13 per 1000 persons. **(NASSCOM, 2002)**

In the area of job creation, according to a survey conducted by the NASSCOM, software industry including user organizations have employed 340,000 professionals as on 31 March 2000 as against 160,000 professionals in 1996. It has been reported that cyberkiosks in India have generated 600,000 jobs under private initiative.

Libraries, Museums and archives are digitizing their resources and services on large scales. Libraries with computerized catalogues are now becoming part of networks. Scores of premier institutions like Indian Institute of Technology(s), (IIT) Indian Institute of Management(s) (IIM) and laboratories under Council for Scientific and Industrial Research (CSIR) are spending huge amounts on digital collections. In national library, Calcutta nearly 750,000 pages have been scanned and stored in CDs under the ongoing schemes for digitizing selected books and old documents. In Central Secretariat Library, New Delhi, the bibliography of rare books in CD-ROM format linking images of the title and content pages is in progress.

Recently , the government has decided to create a Traditional Knowledge Digital Library (TKDL). The purpose is to integrate the widely scattered knowledge in Indian system of medicine. TKDL will comprise of 35,000 formulations collected from 35 texts available in public domain.

## 5. The Digital Revolution: Socio-Human Perspective

Information technology has a potential to revolutionize the government functioning and is vital for the way government serves the people. It offers endless opportunities to bring societal transformation centered on education, healthcare, agriculture and governance leading to higher employment generation, higher industrial growth, higher national efficiency and productivity and higher empowerment of women. By the use of IT multiple technologies can be interwoven to realize a knowledge-propelled society. With India carving a sizeable niche for itself, it is uniquely placed to fully capitalize the emerging opportunities for its socio-economic transformation.

In a country like India where people in the rural areas lack basic amenities like water, sanitation, electricity, and proper roads, Information technology can be used as a tool to mitigate some of the administrative problems. IT can weaken the information asymmetry prevalent in the countryside by providing timely information. In several parts of the country, farmers are beginning to realize how real-time information, made available either through state-sponsored or private initiatives, can help them earn better prices for their crops.

### 6. Important Social Initiatives

As application of IT revolution to rural India can not be left to a single agency, a number of projects have been started in rural areas by both by NGOs and government for providing right information so as to enhance the information literacy. In Madhya Pradesh's Dhar district, for example, villagers get the latest quotations for their potato crop from the state's wholesale markets for as little as Rs.5. In the process, they have found that their average realization has gone up by as much as 33 per cent as middlemen have been done away with.

National Institute of Rural Development, Hyderabad has set up two information kiosks for the villagers. *Drishtee*, an NGO is an organizational platform for developing IT enabled services to rural and semi-urban population through the usage of state-of-the art software. The services include access to government programs and benefits, and market related information. The Tamil Nadu government proposes to set up 13,0000 Community Internet Centers all over the state to provide easy access to computers. From corporate sector, HP Labs India is developing products appropriate for India's rural market. The focus is on making information technology available to those who use Indian languages and making devices affordable. Intel and World Links, with the support of World Economic Forum proposes to launch three larger projects to introduce computers, computer literacy skills and teacher professional development training in disadvantaged, lower middle class secondary schools throughout the country.

Government plays a key role in taking IT to the masses. In the state of Andhra Pradesh, for instance, land records have been totally computerized and every district and village is expected to be networked in the future. A video conference network connects the chief minister with 25 key locations in the state. Other states are following quickly.

Associations, civil societies, self-help groups, NGOs and various foundations have emerged as important stakeholders in this process of development. A series of small-scale IT projects have come up as a result of their initiatives, sometimes with catalytic roles of government. M.S. Swaminathan Research Foundation at Pondicherry in south India runs Village Knowledge Center project using wireless radio for data and voice transmission between semi-urban hub center and village centers. The hub provides connectivity to the Internet through dial-up telephone lines, and the staff there creates locally useful content. The village centers receive queries from the local residents and transmit information, collected from the hub, back to them. An important feature of this project is the strong sense of ownership that the village communities have developed towards the village centers. The other key feature is the active participation of rural women in the management of the village center as well as in using it. **(http:// www.mssrf.org/ information village assessment. htm)**

The Warana Wired Village Project at Maharashtra, the Gyandoot Project at Madhya Pradesh, n-Logue

Communications at work in Tamil Nadu and Rajasthan are other examples of such initiatives to introduce IT for community development.

The Warana Project was jointly executed by NIC, Maharashtra State Government, and the *Warana Vibhag Shikshan Mandal.* (Education Council) The services that include automation of the working of the cooperative societies, and provision of agricultural, medical, and educational information to villagers are provided free. The kiosk manager is appointed by the village *panchayats* (local self government body) as a part-time activity.

The system includes both web-based and Intranet-based applications. The web-based applications are the agriculture produce market information system, agricultural schemes and crop technology information system, computer learning aids, village information systems, educational and vocational guidance systems, government documents and procedures systems, and computerization of the local cooperative market. The Intranet-based systems are the wired management of sugarcane cultivation, land records computerization, the computerization of the Warana Milk Dairy, and a Grievance Registration and Redressal System **(http://www.uncrd)**

There are also similar projects for IT based education, some of which are targeted to the poor. Trahatt.com (www.trahatt.com) developed by Delhi based NGO. Development Alternative is a commercial project to provide online services to rural communities in north India. It has a highly interactive and graphics-intensive interface which allows semi-literate and neo-literates to access the products.

UNICEF along with the Government of Andhra Pradesh and Karnataka has launched a project, *Sisu Samarakshak* (Child Protection) to equip women and children with information and services pertaining to health, nutrition, hygiene and children's care. The multilingual information portal which is at the final stage of its development will provide information on maternal care, child survival development and nutrition and HIV/AIDS. During the next phase of the project the community members will be able to access services such as birth certificates, access land records, order water and sanitation supplies from sanitation marts, purchase agriculture commodities and communicate sub standard service delivery to the local officers and most important, communicate with officials when emergency health services are required. **(UNICEF, 2002)**

The National Dairy Development Board (NDDB) is helping co-operative unions across the country to set up computer systems, connecting the villagers who sell milk to the union office and the union office itself to NDDB. The Board is going to 1,000 villages thus avoiding the middleman through use of computers.

At the milk production center in Anand, Gujarat, women take milk to a weigh-bridge. There the milk is weighed, the fat quantity assessed, and the payment immediately calculated by the computer. Earlier middlemen could cheat saying the fat content was low. Records—right from quantities sold to payrolls—are automatically maintained and are tamper-proof compared to the time-consuming ledger work in the past.

A veterinary doctor in Tiruchi in Tamil Nadu is computerizing all details of animal and poultry diseases. This will be available in booths across the villages in the area, so that people know exactly what should be done for prevention and cure.

In Andhra Pradesh (AP), a professor is working on the prototype of software on animal health care to dispel misinformation and provide villagers with information on animal diseases. Information dissemination would become simple and speedy, with every village in AP expected to have an Internet booth soon. In the Medak district of Andhra Pradesh, a digital database of the medical history of all the families ensures medical facilities for everyone for Rs 100 a year. In Barmer, Rajasthan, the farmers monitor the mandi rates through the net and sell only when the rates are optimal.

A large majority of rural women in India have never seen a telephone or television, and with literacy rate ranging between 8-10 per cent, the Internet revolution is yet to touch their daily lives. Yet we have the example of a rural woman embroiderer, Maniben, from Kutch in Gujarat. A non-profit organization, with help from the National Institute of Fashion Technology (NIFT), featured her mirror-work embroidered tie on its web site—peoplelink.org. Maniben received orders from UK to make "Millennium" ties.

Growth of IT industry has a positive effect on the employment situation in the country. It has generated demand for skilled manpower at various levels of specialization. Semi-skilled and moderately skilled manpower are on demand in various activities involving IT applications like data processing, back-office operation, call centers, medical transcriptions, claims processing (like insurance claims), web designing etc. Demand for skilled manpower is generated in the area of software development, programming and network related operations. In addition, there is demand for trained manpower for after sales service, repair and maintenance of hardware and customer support services in both hardware and software.

The government has sponsored training institutes like Indian Institute of Technology and Management at Gwalior and four other Indian Institutes of Information Technology (at Allahabad, Bangalore, Kolkata and Hyderabad), upgrading regional engineering colleges, encouraging private sector participation in training, giving active support to the polytechnics, colleges and private training institutes in the field of IT and extending accreditation to institutions at the non-formal sector for certain courses by the DOEACC, a society formed for the purpose. Several initiatives have made it possible to use computer in local languages.

### 7. Information for All: Equitable Information Order vs. Digital Deprivation

The big question is, will IT do an encore for India as a nation, and not just for a wafer thin percentage of IT-literate Indians, mostly the poster boys of the IITs?. Asks Dipankar Das. **(Das, 2001)**

The answer is that economic life in rural India, for that matter of the poor in particular, is yet to evolve around IT. IT has not yet touched the lives of the average citizen and India is nowhere close to being much hyped up "knowledge economy or society". The above cited initiatives and projects, if not selective, can largely be described as peripheral in nature. A large section of Indian society is still living in a state of digital deprivation. Despite the urban wealth of hi-tech cities like Bangalore, three quarters of the population still live in villages and deeply entrenched poverty makes the daily struggle to survive a more immediate priority than computer literacy.

As per the International Data Corporation (IDC), survey of 55 countries, India ranks 54th on its Information Society Index. The 2000 World Times/IDC index measures the global impact of IT and Internet adoption and establishes a standard by which all nations are measured according to their ability to assess and absorb information and IT. **(IDC, 2002)**

India's growing digital divide separates a narrow upper crust of "bandwidth-hungry urbanites" from the vast majority of their malnourished, illiterate countrymen, who may have to walk days just to get to the nearest working telephone. The major metropolises are at par with some of the developed countries, but rural areas in states like eastern Bihar and Orissa are worse off than several of the least developed countries. Online banking, online transactions and e-commerce and many other IT related applications are still alien to rural economy.

Groaning under basic problems such as illiteracy, malnutrition and sheer poverty, India's rural populace may as well be living on a planet different from, say, Bangalore, which, according to the United Nations Development Program **(UNDP)** human development report for 2001, is better off than many cities in the United States, Europe and Japan when it comes to technological innovation. The report clearly brought out India's digital divide between a few urban centers and the vast rural hinterland. Among India's 1.4 million Internet connections, more than 1.3 million are cornered by the states of Delhi, southern Karnataka (of which Bangalore is capital), Tamil Nadu and western Maharashtra.

The situation is worse in India's vast rural hinterland. Barely 25 km from New Delhi is India's most populous state Uttar Pradesh which according to U.N. Development Programme estimates will take all of this century to make all its 170 million people literate. **(UNDP, 2001)**

### 8. Digital Divide: Causes, Constraints and Solutions

India being one of the poorest countries in the world with extremely low literacy rates in rural areas, 25 per cent without health services, 71 per cent without access to sanitation, nearly 30 per cent living below the poverty line has extremely powerful inbuilt constraints towards establishing an equitable information order. Huge linguistic diversity, deeply ingrained ideologies of caste-hierarchy, gender inequality and communal divisions further hinder the developmental efforts

Access to technology is further constrained by infrastructure parameters like electricity, the number of personal computers (PCs) and telephone lines. Per capita electricity consumption in India remains around 363 kW, far below the 4,959 kW in Hong Kong, one of the region's technology powerhouses, the 5,421 kW in Britain and the 11,822 kW in the U.S. India has 22 telephone lines per 1,000 people compared with 70 in neighboring China and three PCs per 1,000 compared with nine in China. The installed base of PCs in the country is five million, which means only five out of every 1,000 people have a PC.

When it comes to bringing computers to the masses, it's hard to make progress without government systems. There's limited use for example in giving free computers to village schools if there's no electricity. Internet programs aren't much use without phone connections.

Despite government initiative in promoting rural telephony, tele-density in the rural area is low. By the end of December 2001, there were 7.6 million Direct Exchange Line (DEL) in rural areas meaning thereby availability of 7 phones per 1000 people. The cost of access network is still very high and is not affordable for the population in the low-income group. **(ICTs' 2001).**

### 9. Public Policy: Constraints and Limitations

Privatization of telecommunications pursued since 1994 had brought in investments. But these were concentrated in the profitable urban centers because private players were unwilling to invest in the non-profitable rural areas, where 70 per cent of India's 1 billion people lived. This was a pity because investment in the rural areas could transform the lives of millions of farmers - not only in terms of freeing them from the stranglehold of middleman traders with reliable, real-time market information, but also by getting to them and their families virtually non-existent health care and educational facilities.

This could largely be attributed to India's slow telecommunications expansion to a number of factors, including tight bureaucratic control, poor policies and inadequate investment by private companies and lack of funds of the government, which until recently held monopoly control. Cost in installing backbone communication lines throughout the country is an awesome task. Even if they can somehow manage to buy PCs, maintenance, supplying parts, and training people how to use them are more difficult.

Unfortunately nowhere is the digital divide more glaring than in IT education. India's 'obsession' with the software industry and its export orientation is leading to the churning out of unemployable students on one hand and bright whiz kids on the other. While the latter are lured away by overseas employers, the former remain unemployable. Experts ask for cautions against the 'hype' associated with the phenomenal growth of India's software industry — defying rational explanations and built up into a 'mystique of sort' which breeds false hopes.

This situation itself is a product of the skewed priorities: spending 60 per cent of the education budget to subsidize the IITs and IIMs, while spending the rest on secondary and primary education. "The revolution in information technology (IT), far from helping India to leapfrog to a post-industrial society, threatens to rupture the social fabric by enriching a few at the cost of many". **(Das, 2002)**

## 10. New Possibilities

For bridging digital divide with effective practical applications of technology, three elements are crucial, entreprenuership, government policy encouraging and supporting equity and ground level programs with local community participation. A significant proportion of India's population belongs to the traditionally backward communities and a process of computer education, particularly focussed on these groups is required. By developing of relevant software for interaction in regional languages and through pictures and icons to enable illiterates acquire information.

There is a need for establishing rural information networks which will allow knowledge, services, money, and certain kinds of information products to flow easily across long distances, from one public access information center to another. Each village node might have multiple institutional identities, serving as a virtual community center, bank, medical resource, government counter, matrimonial bureau, public library and educational resource center all at once.

An urgent requirement in this direction is to break the barrier of language so as to provide content in local languages. In a country where nearly 70 per cent of the population is working in agriculture sector it is very important that contents are relevant to the agricultural economy. By enhancing access to education and health care through distance learning and tele-medicine, IT can improve the quality of life for poor rural communities who do not have access to these facilities. The Indian fishing village of Veerampatinam in Tamil Nadu is a case in point, where weather forecasts downloaded from the Internet and broadcast by loud speakers at the beach enabled the poor fishermen to know better when to venture into the sea in their boats for fishing. Similarly the public call booths dotting the countryside in Bangladesh only go to show how the poor rural communities in developing countries can access the state-of-the-art telecommunications without owning any equipment, per se.

## 11. Conclusion

Tremendous gains have been made by the computerization of the government functioning, not only in strengthening the delivery of existing services but also by improving policy planning and implementation through more effective provision of information to policy makers. The direct and immediate benefits of use of IT in Government are improvements in service quality, efficiency and government-people relationships by providing quick, easy and transparent access to information.

There is an urgent need to target basic needs such as primary education, basic health services, water and sanitation requirements particularly in rural and backward areas. The new ICT applications and content relevant to the demand in rural areas, can drastically improve the delivery of information related services to people in general and agriculture extension services and provision of health and social services in rural areas in particular.

The policymakers must take into consideration the broader picture when designing IT policy and treat it as a part of an overall economic strategy in which sound economic policies will benefit IT sector and diffusion of IT will have positive effects on economic development and social welfare. Formation of partnerships between local bodies, the local administration and NGOs appears to hold the key. Development of applications, such as an online system for community banking, will contribute to the economic sustainability of the operations. It will also go a long way to humanize and sensitize Indian information revolution.

## References

Das (Dipankar). Great Indian digital divide. at http://www.hindustantimes.com/nonfram/290600/detOPI03.htm http://www.uncrd

ICTs' (2001). ICTs in rural poverty alleviation. Economic and Political Weekly. 36(11), 917-920.

India, Department of Electronics(1988). Policy on computer software exports, software development and training , New Delhi.

India, Department of Electronics, Government of India. 'New Computer Policy'. Electronics Information and Planning, 12.(2).89 - 94

India, Ministry of Commerce and Industry. Export & Import Policy. 2000.

India, Planning Commission(2002). Approach paper to tenth five year plan.

India, Science & Technology (Department of). A draft paper for a new technology policy. New Delhi. 1993.

India, Ministry of Information & Broadcasting. IT Act 2000. at www.mit.gov.in/it-bill.htm

NASSCOM (2002). The IT in India: Strategic Review . New Delhi, pp. 21-22.

NASSCOM (2002). The IT in India: Strategic Review. New Delhi, pp. 54.

NASSCOM (2002). The IT in India: Strategic Review. New Delhi, pp. 67.

UNICEF Newsletter. Children in India. November 2002.

United Nations Development Program Human Development Report for year 2001.

www.apnic.net/mailing-lists/s-asia-it/archive/2000/08/msg00007.html

www.mssrf.org

www.trahatt.com

# 12

# Serials Management and Control System: Need for a Computerised Approach

## 1. Introduction

The significance of serials as a means of transmission of knowledge has increased manifold since World War II. The magnitude of serial publications provide ample proof of the growing recognition of their importance. They constitute about 75% of all publications and according to B.C. Vickery in 1965 there were 850,000 articles in the 26,000 periodicals held by British Library Landing Division (BLLD).[1] Lancaster estimates that during 1977 some 50,000 scientific journals were being published.[2] Osborn using data from the Library of Congress states that by 1957, 630,000 serial publications had at some time or place been published since the first printed newspaper in 1609. His estimate for 1971 was 900,000 serials, with a projected figure of 1.5 million serials by the year 2000.[3] According to Katz there are now about 100,000 scientific and technical periodicals which publish over two million articles each year.[4]

## 2. Definition of a serial

A Serial may broadly be defined as a publication in a continuous series, with a consecutive number and no predetermined end, as distinct from a single work in several parts. ALA Glossary of library terms defines serial as "A publication issued in successive parts usually at regular intervals, and as a rule intended to be continued indefinitely. Serials include periodicals, annuals (reports, yearbook, etc.) and memoirs, proceedings and transactions of societies".[5] According to AACR2 a serial is "A publication in any medium issued in successive parts bearing numerical chronological designations and intended to be continued indefinitely. Serials include periodicals; newspapers; annuals (reports, yearbooks, etc); the journals, memoirs, proceedings, transactions, etc., of societies; and numbered monograph series.[6] Ranganathan made a distinction between 'serial' and periodical 'publication'. He defined serial as a "periodical publication of which each volume or each periodical group of volume; embodies more or less the same kind of information usually in the same pattern, mainly relating to its year (or other period) of coverage. It is usually released complete as a volume. It is not made of diverse contributers, each forming a comprehensive exposition of knowledge".[7]

## 3. Management of Serials

Serial work is entirely a problem area. By nature serials are individual, erratic and unpredictible. Their selection, acquisition, check-in, cataloguing and even public service constitute a difficult assignment. The routines involved are incessant; their price, title, publisher, frequency and scope are subject to change. Serials merge or split, get suspended for varying lengths of time. Even serial numbering is a fertile area for confusion and chaos.

### 3.1 *Acquisition of Serials*

A collection development policy of serials is particularly important because they are harder to select and demand more critically informed selection choices. A mistake breeds serious financial implications. According to Osborn, selection of a periodical is an art. Its skilled performance depends primarily on the exercise of trained informed judgement. He has laid down some general guiding principles in this regard described as below:

(a) Acquire the material which open up the literature of a subject or a country.

(b) As far as possible specimen copy should be acquired before it is regularly subscribed.

(c) Duplication of periodicals should be avoided.

(d) A complete set should be maintained instead of a broken set.

(e) There should be co-ordination in maintaining the titles of periodicals at least in the place or region where a university library is functioning for preservations of local publications.

(f) In research libraries allocate an amount for acquiring back files of periodicals.[8]

The above guiding principles can be of use in the selection of periodicals though actual practice of selection varies from one type of library to another. Academic and special libraries in USA have increasingly sought to employ subject experts as bibliographers or selection officers. Vickery[9] has made an important study in regard to recognizing the most significant periodical literature. The strategy evolved by him is based on following basis approaches:

(a) The analysis of records compiled for other purposes, e.g. reference counts of citations at the ends of papers.

(b) Diaries and questionnaires to be completed by users at the actual time of reading sample items of literature.

(c) Questionnaires recording user's opinions and estimate of their reading.

### 3.2 *Selection Aids and Tools*

The following are some of the important tools which should be consulted as they are immensely helpful for acquisition purpose and provide sufficient bibliographic and reference service.

(a) Ulrich's International Periodicals Directory: a classified guide to a selected list of current periodicals. New York, R R Bowker.

(b) World List of Scientific Periodicals. New York.

(c) Guide to Current British Periodicals. London, Library Association.

(d) New Serial Titles, 1961 to-date, Washington D C, Library of Congress.

(e) Standard Periodicals Directory 1964 to-date. New York, Oxbridge.

(f) British Union Catalogue of Periodicals; a record of periodicals of the world from the seventeen century to the present day in British Libraries, London, Butterworths.

(g) Serial Titles Newly Received (Library of Congress)

(h) Times Literary Supplement. Under "Current Periodicals" columns.

(i) Aslib Information Guide.

### 3.3 *Serial Acquisition System*

Serial acquisition and ordering is the most difficult phase of serials management. Basically there are six means of acquiring serials to libraries:

(a) By purchase from a local book shop or news agents.

(b) By subscription to publishers of the periodicals who mail copies directly to the libraries

(c) By dealing with the vendors/agents

(d) By taking the membership of the learned society or professional body.

(e) By gift

(f) By exchange programme

Among all these methods, the most prevalent way is to subscribe serials directly from publishers. The periodicals are promptly delivered and economies in the form of multiyear subscription at reduced rates are sometimes possible.

The libraries which take large numbers of periodicals more often contact agents to supply periodicals. Invoices are obtained from the various agencies and the vendors who quote lowest rate is asked to undertake the supply. The chief advantage of this system is saving of time and labour. The agent is responsible for the efficient handling of renewals, to ensure continuity and will look after all claims. He will provide information on new and obscure periodicals and will also supply price quotations, subject list and catalogues. Amount for subscription can be paid with one bill once a year at any time. However, some times the agents delay the remittance of subscription amount to the respecive publishers for earning thousands of rupees of interest on the advance amount paid by the libraries. This malpractice affects the timely and regular supply of periodicals.

### 3.4 *Order work*

Before the start of a new financial year or new calendar year Librarian should prepare a list of periodicals to be subscribed duly approved by the concerned authority. It is to be ensured that the total amount of subscription fee does not exceed that sanctioned fund.

Vendors should not ordinarily be changed very often and vendors should be informed well before time that such and such periodicals are to be renewed so that the relevant issues are received without interruption or delay. The vendors should also be informed simultaneously about the cancellation of journals if any.

### 3.5 *Serials Recording*

It is essential to record with care the arrival of every

issue or periodicals or serials subscribed to and of any special issues, indexes, volume, title page or other material regularly accompanying them. This phase of serials management is important since these record notes are the basic evidence against which the library checks invoices before payment and in case of inordinate delay in receipt of any issue, it helps to take followup action. In case of non-receipt of any issue a reminder must be sent to the supplier as soon as a gap in the sequence of issues is detected without any explanation or information from the publishers. The entire claiming system, therefore, depends upon the library's knowing the approximate date of arrival for each serial. It is also necessary to keep a record of claims so that the work is not duplicated.

### 3.6 *Serials Recording Methods*

The most critical aspect of serials work is the daily recording of serials, periodicals and newspapers received. The basic recording method is to maintain a unit control record for each title. This can be a page in a note book, register, ledger, a card or a slip in a visible index also called Kardex or a computer record. For small libraries subscribing to a dozen or a score or periodicals, register system is more suitable. The periodicals may be entered in the register in an alphabetical manner. The date of its receipt is entered in the month column against the periodicals in question and similar date is given on the title over the periodical.

Kardex is not portable and sometimes the cards are lost or wear out. But cards can be manipulated easily and they are relatively cheaper also. Ranganathan's three cards system is very useful for the complete maintainence of bound volumes also but is considered complex and a bit cumbersome.

### 3.7 *Routing of Serials*

By routing of serials is meant the assistance given by the library to the users in making available the articles or the periodicals itself on demand. The process usually entails the use of serials records, bibliographic tools and the serials themselves. The entire exercise consists of reference and a variety of other functions administered not only by the periodical section but by various units. A library is supposed to undertake the following services for the efficient public service in this regard:

3.7.1 *Circulation*

To render possible satisfactory service different libraries have adopted different types of methods of periodical circulation. The first simple method is to issue the periodicals to one member of staff who has to pass it on to other turn by turn without the need of returning to the library each time. A routing slip may be attached on the cover page containing detailed instructions as regard to the duration and the order of further circulation.

3.7.2 *Group routing method*

This method is adopted in research or academic libraries and periodicals are issued to group of readers preferably belonging to one section or department within one organization. It is further circulated by the members of the group among themselves and on a fixed date it has to be returned to the library.

3.7.3 *Department issue method*

The periodicals pertaining to a particular subject or department are transferred to the concerned department which keeps the issue for a longer period, generally upto the time when the volume is completed and then it is returned to the library for binding and record.

### 3.8 *Indexing and Abstracting Work*

An index of periodical is a systematically arranged list giving information about each items so as to enable it to be identified and traced easily. A library can provide the following types of indexes with regard to the contents of a periodical:

### 3.8.1 *The content page service*

The most basic analysis of contents of a particular periodicals issue is the list of contents usually provided on a page close to the front of issue. The content pages of the journals can be photocopied and circulated among the users so as to enable them to know the article(s) of their interest.

### 3.8.2 *Index to Individual Periodicals*

All the received journals in the library should be fully indexed according to their respective subjects. The author of the articles and the country of the coverage of the article should also be identified to facilitate retrospective literature searching.

### 3.8.3 *Abstracting Service*

Today's user has neither time nor to go through the entire literature available on the subject of his interest. Library can provide the abstract of the various articles to enable the reader to select the most important material quickly. As compared to indexes, abstracts are likely to increase the accuracy in literature selection.

## 3.9 *Reference Service*

A large number of reference questions are answered by means of serial publications. The library and the users find needed information from the reference stock of reading material which are by definition serials, volumes in serial sets or government publications. Serial reference work, therefore, is not confined to the location of serial title within the library or without, it also involves the interpretation of citation given in abbreviated, obscure or translated form. The boundary of reference work is extended to the acquisition or location of translation of journal articles, and union list operation connected with inter library lending and procurement of photocopies and in some cases guiding the patrons to the relevant outline database etc. These activities require for the reference librarian to have first hand knowledge of the periodicals themselves, and the indexing and abstracting services for the location of desired periodical articles available at national and international levels.

### 3.10 *Binding of Serials*

Binding is very expensive but an essential phase of serials collection development policy. Commercial binding is the most widely used method of preserving serials. There are number of valid advantages in binding periodicals if they are to be kept for any length or time in store. Unbound parts are bulky, difficult to handle and easily misplaced and damaged. Unbound periodicals emit messy look and remain untidy. On the other hand bound volumes are easier to move round the library, they are less bulky and they can be titled and shelf marked on their spines for ease of accurate replacement in sequence. They are easier to refer to and there is no risk of losing the index, if it is bound into the volume.

#### 3.10.1 *When to Bind*

The appropriate time for binding serials varies according to both library priorities and subject of the material. A library may like to bind whenever the volume is complete even sacrificing users' immediate access for sake of security of material. Some libraries make efforts to have certain subject categories of journals available at a particular time. Thus binding policies and their details are unlimited and each library should determine the point of time to send journals to the bindery by considering such variables as public service, security cycle of use, budget and binder's schedule. The written policy should not be too rigid but incorporate enough flexibility to account for unexpected situations.

### 3.10.2 *Binding Preparations*

The essential routine work may include collecting pieces of a title (issues) to form a volume, arranging them in numerical order, top to bottom, securing them temporarily with cotton string, tape, or rubber bands; marking the bundle so that the binder can identify the title; and recording that the volume is being bound. These things should be done according to guidelines which support the library's public service and collection development objectives. The guidelines will vary from library to library.

It is the duty of binding assistant to check and determine that the volumes are complete and tied together in correct manner before he prepares binding slip. The form that accompanies a serial volume to the bindery may be produced manually or computerized. It is also essential for the binding assistant to record at every appropriate location the titles and volumes that are at the bindery and the date they left the library. This information is needed at public service point in serials department if a library has, if not, the patrons would like to get information from central circulation desk. Whichever location is used, it is important that library staff member must know where to direct patrons to confirm that a specific volume is at the bindery. When this record is kept within the serials department, it is possible also to record the date of return from the bindery. This information can help locate a recently bound serial which may travel through a number of checkpoints before it reaches its place in the stacks.

## 3.11 *Cataloguing of Serials*

The serial function can be seriously impaired if they are not properly catalogued as it is an important tool for bibliographic control also. The cataloguing provides a uniform medium for arrangement of serials entries in a charging system in libraries which circulate serial publications and also allow serials to be found systematically. Whether a library follows the AACR or any other code, whether it gives detailed cataloguing, with complete classification or not, the point is this: adequate bibliographic control of serial is an absolute must. Cataloguing is key to this bibliographic control. Without it, there is naught but chaos. Serials also need to be properly catalogued in order to faciliate co-operative ventures like union list. Adequate interlibrary loan can not exist without catalogued serials.

Cataloguing of serials consists mainly of two processes: descriptive cataloguing and subject cataloguing. Descriptive cataloguing consists of two elements: descriptive and physical work. The physical description of works starts with the title and ends with the notes. The purpose of description is to establish the work's identity.

The main entry of a serial generally comprises the following eight descriptive elements:

Title and/Statement of Responsibility Areas.

Edition.

Numeric and/or Alphabetic, Chronological, or other Description Area.

Publication, Distribution, etc., Area.

Physical Description Area.

Series Area.

Note Area.

Standard Number (ISSN) key-title and terms of availability Area.

### 4. Computer Based Serials Control System

To combat and control the bizarre world of serials, computer has emerged as a very effective tool. In the beginning it was considered one of the most difficult house keeping operations to be automated, but today computerized serials control is widely replacing the manual system. The basic requirements of serials system are similar to, but tedious than those for controlling a collection of monographs.[10]

The majority of computer-based serials systems are designed to produce lists in various orders, such as title, subject, location or supplier and include the sub-systems:

### 4.1 *Inventory*

Inventories of serials may be prepared primarily in the card form under the title and the subject with cross references from previous files, if any. Each title is recorded by the date of the first volume and subsequent volumes indicating the issues missing if any. Location is indicated by the call number given to periodical title or the shelf mark.

### 4.2 *Ordering and Acquisition*

The initial ordering for a serial is akin to ordering a monograph. Ordering entails like requesting, approving, checking, ordering and accounting in respect of each new serial title. Details of price, cost invoice, amount paid or ready for payment are recorded.

The acquisitions function may be divided into two parts i.e., receiving and claiming. When an issue is received, it must be checked to ensure that this is the correct or latest item received and then the main data file must be amended to show new receipts. Typically a file of punched cards is created for all the serials to be received in batch system. When the issue arrives the card file is searched and extracted and a new card prepared if no appropriate card is present in the file. All cards relevant to the issues received are eventually processed in a batch and the computer-held main data file is updated. The remaining cards, if any, serve to alert the librarian to the non-receipt of certain issues.

The claiming function is a smaller but a complex job. The point at which the claiming procedures should start, mainly depends upon the professional judgement of the librarian. The computer easily provides list of outstanding issue that the librarian needs in order to send claims.

Preparing record for renewal of subscription is a routine job. The data file for acquisitions may include the details of the dates when subscriptions fall due to be renewed and the amounts to be paid. The printouts of such records may be produced at regular intervals for perusal and action. Renewals notices may be printed by the computer. After making payment in each case of renewal, the account to show balance should be updated. Computer can provide printed lists of the financial situation which are a useful management tool.

### 4.3 *Accessioning*

Each new issue of the serial is recorded in the library. If it is a new serial, it should be put to the data file with bibliographic detail. When all the records are input and the files are updated, the issue may be sent to the reading room or the place where to send.

### 4.4 *Cataloguing*

In an automated serials Cataloguing Work, the bibliographic data is recorded in machine-readable form. As stated before computer-based serials system generates, from the master file, lists in several order, e.g., title, subject, location, supplier etc. Here, there is no difference between a monograph and serial automated work.

The content and format of the serial bibliographic record varies considerably between the local and integrated system. Physical description is mostly based on the eight areas as envisaged in AACR2 or ISBD(S).

### 4.5 *Binding*

The computer-based bindery control modules are either part of an automated check-in system or a stand alone (local) bindery control system. Each bindery system works slightly different. In all cases, however, binding slips or lists are produced to accompany the volumes to be sent to the bindery. These binding slips and/or lists are created from records which generally contain the following data: title (or author and title), binding colour, class of binding, colour of lettering and its style, size and location (for title, volume, and call number), instructions for handling advertisements, indexes, and title page. Most of the systems have the binding data coded in fixed length fields. Some bindry records also contain issue frequency, number of issues bound together, and binding frequency.

The identification of the volumes to be bound can be accomplished automatically using the frequency and the number of issues bound together or using the frequency of binding.

The third function of a bindery control system is to provide a record of volumes at the bindery. This record is made accessible by call number and title as well as the bindery shipment.

All these subsystems must be integrated in one serials control system. Each of the subsystems must have a main file or master file and other working files. All these files must be integrated in one file in the serials control system and all other files and records are subordinate to this core file. The central control, data record, decision making, management production of printouts in desired sequences, accounts statistics and every routine and management job will be controlled by this system with the core file. It may be designated Master Serial Control File. It will hold all the records centrally with connections to the following data files-selection data, ordering data, acquisition data, accessioning data, cataloguing data, description data, circulation data etc.

## 5. International Computarised Serial Control System

Computerization in libraries has created immense potentialities in standardization of data at the international level and opened up a new vista for transfer of and access to information and documents. The capabilities of the computer have been increased enormously. All these situations have contributed to making transfer of software packages across geographical barriers and national boundaries. Attempts have been made for controlling data at the international level by the machine-readable form. Some of the standards evolved over the years by different agencies are as follows:

### 5.1 *ISBD (S)*

To create and maintain international standards in bibliographic descriptions for easy flow of information. IFLA started the programme of the International Standard Bibliographic Description (ISBD) to be applied to national bibliographies, library catalogues and other information sources. The aim of ISBD is to provide standard descriptions for library materials of different kinds, and to ensure international propagation of bibliographic information. The functions of ISBD's are to make records from different sources interchangeable, so that, records produced in one country can be easily accepted in library catalogues and/ or other bibliographic lists in any other country and to assist in the interpretation of records transcending language barriers, so that records produced for users of one language can be interpreted by users of other languages.

### 5.2 *ISSN*

For identification, ordering and processing of serial publications, the International Standard Serial Number (ISSN) is being used. It consists of seven digits, plus one check digit and a code with no meaning. The digits are sequential and the system is hospitable to all serials, continuing or ceased. There are many national centres established in different countries, and they register and allocate the International Standard Serial Numbers. These unique International Standard Serial Numbers (ISSNs) facilitate computerization of serials catalogue records by providing machine-readable serials records. These ISSNs act as access point to the international network of serials publications. They also promote computer-based information service on the strength of holdings of serials in various libraries at the international level.

### 5.3 *CODEN*

ISSN is not the only serial numbering system. Twenty-year older is CODEN system developed by the American Society for Testing and Materials, fully titled CODEN for Periodical titles.[11] It is controlled by the Chemical Abstracts Service and covers mainly scientific and technical literature.

### 5.4 *ISDS*

The International Serial Data System (ISDS) was set up in 1971 under the world science infomation programme. UNISIST, recognizing the fact that an internationally accepted coding system for serials was essential for machine-readable records. The general aims of the ISDS are to :[12]

(a) Develop and maintain an international register of serial publications.

(b) Define and promote the use of international standard serial numbers.

(c) Facilitate the retrieval of scientific and technical information in serials.

(d) Make this information currently available to all countries, organizations or individual users.

(e) Establish a communications network between libraries, secondary information services, publishers of serial literature and international organizations.

(f) Promote international standards for bibliographic descriptions communication formats, and information exchange in the area of serials publications.

Details of serials are reported to the international centre in Paris by the forty-five or so national centres which are situated all over the world.

Thus it can be seen that serial control system has become well-entranched even at international level. Efforts are on to devise more meaningful formats so as to make the control system more effective.

## 6. Conclusion

The exponential growth of serial literature has immensly enhanced the need to evolve an effective and fool-proof serial control and management system. Given the chaotic and erratic nature of serials, the serial librarian has to be on his toes-always guarding against any possible discrepency leading to the disruption in the entire system. The need to establish an impregnible control method becomes all the more necessary due to the prohibitory exorbitant prices of serials. This is further multiplied by the fact that all serious scholars and user harbour a protective feeling towards them. To honour these feelings an era of resource crunch library has to resort to resource sharing on large scale. No meaningful resource sharing can take place without proper bibliographic control. The use of computer has come to play a vital role in this respect. It facilitates a free and fast flow of information. The need for effective serial control system has been recognised at international level and several agencies are engaged in designing and formulating a generalised format and standard so as to undertake the venture of resource sharing at international footing.

## References

1. Vickery (BC), Statistics of Scientific and Technical Articles, *Journal of Documentation*. 24; 193-8, 1968.

2. Lancaster (F W). Towards Paperless Information System. 1978. Academic Press, New York, p. 66.
3. Osborn (Andrew). Serial Publications: Their Price and Treatment in Libraries. Ed 3. 1980. American Library Association, Chicago, p. 25.
4. Katz (William). Introduction to reference work, Ed. 5. 1987. McGraw Hills, New York, p. 31.
5. A L A Glossary of library and information science. 1983 American Library Association, Chicago, p. 203.
6. Anglo American Cataloguing Rules. Ed. 2. 1978 The Library Association, London. p. 570.
7. Ranganathan (S R). Prolegomina to library classification Ed 3. 1967. Asia Publishing House, Bombay, p. 212.
8. Osborn. Op cit. P. 81.
9. Vickery (B C) Use of scientific literature, *Library Association Record*, 63; 1975; 263-269.
10. Tedd (Lucy A). An introduction to computer based library systems. Ed 2. 1984. John Wiley, New York, p. 162-163.
11. Mahapatra (Piyushkant). Computer in library science. 1985. World Press, Calcutta, pp. 89-91.
12. Tedd. *Op cit.*, p. 162.

# 13

# An Overview of Some Selected Information Products and Resources

## 1. Introduction

The profound changes that are taking place in the information and communication technology have permeated all walks of life. Being no exception to this, librarians are at the forefront in the integration of new technologies into their services. Libraries have realized that there is a need to organize the information sources available electronically so that users can find resources for their research, teaching and consultancy services.

Rapid developments in technology facilitated the origin of new electronic devices, media and formats. Libraries with a vision are trying to accommodate all types of media and providing services to their clientele in a more convenient and efficient way. Though electronic sources cannot fully replace the printed collections but can definitely augment these collections.

The digital information resources are going to play most vital role in the 21st century. Research centres and individual all over the world generate information in digital form on the Internet.

## 2. Types of Digital Resources

Digital refers to any resource, which is in digitized form i. e. which can be read and scanned by means of electronic media. Like conventional forms digitized resources do not require separate space in a library as this can be stored in a computer locally and remotely. Digital resources include range of material such as:

(I) Collection in which complete contents of documents are created or converted in to machine readable form for online access.

(II) Online databases and CD-ROM information products particularly those with multimedia and interactive video components.

(III) Computer storage devices such as optical disk, juke boxes, CD-ROM/DVD-ROM

(IV) Databases accessible through Internet and other networks

(V) One option of acquisition of digital resource is digitizing existing important and useful print material, it also helps in preserving rare and fragile objects without denying accesses to those to study.

(VI) Link and pointers, resources which are freely available on the Internet and can be added to libraries catalogues and network resources.

In many cases these material are not "physically owned" by the library in the same sense that printed book or journal may be owned, but instead the library has acquired specific access right to the material on behalf of library clientele. Some of the important electronic products and resources are described below.

## 3. Business Management Journals

### 3.1 *EBSCO*

EBSCO is a international database covering all the

disciplines. This full text bibliographic data base is very useful resource in business and management environment. Ebsco offers access to more than 8,000 e-journals and over 3.6 million full-text articles. The journals and information are mostly collected from the famous technical publishers like Elsevier and Black-Well and also information from the international technical societies directly. .

### 3.2 *Proquest on-line journals*

Promoted by Proquest, ABI / INFORM and Business periodicals on disc, and online provides extensive material on variety of business topics including , Market conditions and strategy; Management trends and corporate culture; Corporate case studies; Company news and analysis; International trade and investment; Economic conditions and forecasts.

Material is available in the form of full image articles, citations and 25-150 word abstracts. Subscription provides material for the current year and a three-year back-file, with updates provided monthly. The full image capability means users can view and retrieve exact article copies appearing just as they do in the original publication. ABI/ INFORM and Business Periodicals On disc (BPO) is available in two editions: i) Global Editions: Abstracting and indexing from around 1,520 titles in ABI/Inform Global edition with page images from over 630 titles and searchable full text from 730 sources in BPO Global editions. This edition was compiled specifically to meet the research needs of international users. By bringing together information from hundreds of key international journals, BPO Global edition enables users to track business trends and activity in all industry sectors around the world; ii) Research Edition: Abstracting and indexing from over 1,270 titles in ABI/Inform Research edition with page images from 470 titles in BPO Research edition cover subjects like Accounting, Banking, Business, Computers, Economics, Energy, Engineering, Environment, Finance, Healthcare,

Human Resources, International Trends, Insurance, Law, Management, Marketing, Medicine, Public Administration, Taxation, Telecommunications.

Searching the Database: BPO uses the popular ProQuest search ware. ProQuest is powerful and easy to use regardless of users' computer knowledge or search expertise. There are two ways to search the database i.e free text searching and multiple indexes to help users avoid the trial and error guessing the correct term. Indexed terms are available for – companies, subjects, geographic places, journals, authors, key words and industry sectors.

BPO has the unique opportunity to combine a rapid search across hundreds of journals with immediate delivery of the original documents. It provides organizations with an instant electronic journal collection, including a huge archive. This in turn reduces many costs associated with journal storage and binding. In addition, BPO journals are unaffected by problems of theft and mutilation, nor are there the frustrations and cost of obtaining articles from outside via inter library loans.

Four major areas are very informative and effective.

3.2.1 *Toc Premier*

Covering information on 23,000 journals and nearly 80 million records available in citations only database. Toc Premier is covering all functional areas of management discipline. Most of the information is in abstract form.

The second product of academic research premier is covering general information on all the fields. 3,500 scholarly publications, includes 2,600 pre reviewed publications. In addition to the full text, the data base covers indexing abstracting of 1450 journal collections. This collection is mainly social science, humanities, education, and computer science. The coverage of management discipline is very less.

### 3.2.2 *Business source premier*

This database covers only the business and management information. 2,800 full-text scholarly publications include 900 pre reviewed journals and 3,350 of indexing and abstracting information. This database offers information in all areas of business and management like, Marketing, finance, human resource etc.

## 3.3 *Blackwell Synergy*

Blackwell publisher is one of the world's largest publishers with a total of over 600 prestigious journals from the international association, societies within the physical science, social science, medicine and humanities. All Blackwell journals are available online as well as in print editions. Online journals can be accessed through black-well synergy the online service of the Black-Wells.

The online journal collection is covering all areas of the subjects. In the business and management disciplines their broad terms are business economics, finance accounting, maths and Statistics. The complete full-text and bibliographic information given in the journal database are in the form of PDF and HTML.

The articles and journal collections are taken from the 23 International societies and organizations in the field of business and management.

## 3.4 *Science Direct*

Science Direct is a collection of information resource for millions of scientific works around the world. It is a web database of Elsevier Science publishers. The collections are in multi disciplinary content source including research journals. It covers more than 1,700 scientific and technical journals and 3 million articles and also reports are made available. Access to abstract of article and journal table of content is free for all users.

The Elsevier science publishes all publications in online forms in the name of Science Direct Web Editions. More number of journals articles and reports cover the business and management. Broad areas of the collections are business management and accounting, Economics, Econometrics and Finance. Nearly 300 journals cover these areas.

### 3.5 *Kluwer Online*

Kluwer is one of the leading publishers of online resource covering about 750 journals in subject including science, technology, humanity and management. The collections are divided in to online journals, e-books and e-reference works. Some of the journals are added in pro Quest online information service.

## 4. Electronic Business Information Sources

### 4.1 *Internet Securities Inc.*

ISI Emerging Markets provides full-text news articles, financial statements, Industry analyses, equity quotes etc. It covers about 600 information sources, critical information on developing economies in Central and Eastern Europe, Asia and Latin America is delivered direct to the subscribers' desktops.

It covers daily news from primary local sources, corporate profiles, financial statements, industry and analyst reports, capital markets quotes, indices, updates and historical information, Macroeconomic statistics and forecasts, Information on legal and regulatory codes, politics and current events.

ISI mainly covers data from the daily newspapers, industry associations, ICRA, CMIE, Kensource (IPO monitor), Powerline reports, USDA, Minerals & Metals Review, Wadhera Industry Publications, Investext reports. The URL is **www.securities.com**.

### 4.2 *Profound*

Profound is another comprehensive international online database on business & industry which is marketed by the Matrix Information Services in India and uses InfoSort for retrieval purposes. Profound includes the following databases:

Researchline: 45,000 research reports from the world's top publishers including EIU

Brokerline: 250,000 analyst reports from over 400 financial institutions

Countryline: Economic analysis on 192 countries from the world's leading research house including EIU country reports.

Companyline: Financial reports on over 4.5 million companies

Briefings: Briefings on 22,000 companies, 1,500 markets and 150 countries

The monthly charges are about $ 400 and one is charged for each additional document download. The web-site for this database is **www.profound.com**.

### 4.3 *IBID*

IBID from Informatics (India) Pvt Ltd. is a business and industry database giving references and abstracts of the articles published in different journals, newspapers, and magazines. IBID is available with a powerful search engine SPIRS of Silver Platter which works on DOS and Windows platforms.

The International weeklies covered include:

Advertising Age, US

Asian Business, Hong Kong

Automotive News, US

Chemical Marketing Reporter, US

Engineering Markest Week, US

Far Eastern Economic Review, Hong Kong

The Lancet, UK

Oil and Gas Journal, US

Plastic News, US

The Economist, UK

The monthlies include:

Advertising Age International, US

Drug and Cosmetic Industry, US

Far East Focus, UK

Global Investor

Market Asia Pacific, US

Plastics and Rubber Asia, UK

The Banker, UK

Leather, US & UK

It also covers almost all the major daily newspapers, weekly & fortnightly magazines and journal like Express Computers, Express Pharma Pulse, Chemical Weekly, Computers Today, Business Today, Business India and so on. The annual subscription is about Rs. 25,000.

### 4.5 *Reuters Business Briefing (RBB)*

One of the products of Reuters is Reuters Business Briefings which is an archive of data on economies, industries and other related topics. Apart from Reuter's news, it covers over 4000 global sources from across the world. Some of the sources covered by RBB are :

Economic Times

India Today

Business World

Auto India

Business India

Hindu

Times of India

Hindustan Times

Business Standard

Business Today

Capital Market

Minerals and Metals Review

Besides above sources, it also covers reports from EIU, FT, New York Times, Business Wires, BBC Monitoring Service, Asia Intelligence Wire, Economist, Forbes, Fortune etc.

### 4.6 *INFAC*

INFAC is another agency providing industry reports on various sectors. The Industries covered by INFAC include:

Automobiles

Chemicals

Oil and Gas

Metals

Textiles

Service Industries

Infrastructure etc.

Besides the industry reports INFAC brings out a useful monthly 'Price Watch' giving the domestic and internation prices for about 100 major commodities, its landed costs, the drivers of price changes, demand-supply expectations etc. The annual subscription for all the industry sectors is about Rs. 4 lakh.

### 4.7 *Products from CMIE (Centre for Monitoring Indian Economy)*

CMIE estabilshed in 1976 is a Bombay based company dealing in economic and business information products. CMIE has four major products namely EIS, Prowess, India Trades and Capex.

(a) **EIS (Economic Intelligence Service):** This service features a series of documents which provide facts about the Indian economy with analysis of the trends and their impact. It contains the statistical data on most of the sectors of the Indian Economy. The important sectors covered include Industry, Foreign Trade, Agriculture, Corporate Sector, National Income, Infrastructure, Capital Markets, Banking & Finance and so on. The annual subscription is Rs. 24,000.

(b) **Prowess:** Prowess is a database of corporates containing about 7000 Indian companies. The database provides financial statements, ratio analysis, funds flows, product profiles, etc. The database is complemented with software tools to enable querying and research. The annual subscription is Rs. 50,000 (standalone version) and Rs. 7,000 (for LAN version).

(c) **India Trades:** India trade provides India's foreign trade statistics from Directorate General of Commercial Intelligence & Statistics (DGCIS) and a variety of related data from its integrated database. The software attached to it enables quick and easy access to the data. The annual subscription costs Rs. 50,000 (standalone version) and Rs. 65000 (LAN version).

(d) **Capex:** CapEx is a database on new and ongoing investment activities in India. An investment project becomes a part of the CapEx database from its inception through its commissioning. The database includes about 4,500 projects. The annual subscription is Rs. 30000 (standalone version) and Rs. 40000 (LAN version).

## 4.8 *Capital Market*

Capital Market provides the financial data on over 10,000 Indian companies. The database provides financial statements, ratio analysis, funds flows, product profiles, etc. The database is complemented with software tools to enable querying and research.

Capital Market also produced the 'News Captions Archives' which contains the compilation of all news articles published in the major financial newspapers and magazines. The web-site for Capital Market is **www.capitalmarket.com** where it regularly provides the stock quotes and news about the primary market.

## 4.9 *Praxis Consulting & Information Services Pvt Ltd.*

Praxis brings out a number of publications on Primary Market. Some of them are listed below:

Prime-Alert: This service from Praxis provides information on the forthcoming Public and Rights Issues. It helps the individual and the institutional investors to plan for their investments into the capital market. It is available on floppies in menu-driven format in dbase and covers about 3273 companies from June 1989 to March 1998. Each entry has the following fields which are also searcheable:

- Company name
- Address, Phone numbers etc.
- Type of Issue
- Issue Amount
- Expected Month of Issue

- Filed with SEBI month
- Brief Project Description
- Project Cost
- Industry
- Lead Managers
- Zone
- OTC Listing
- NRI Preferential Quota
- Issue Opening Date
- Action Taken

The above data can be updated by the user and he can also create new records. Frequency of this service is fortnight. The subscriber also gets the hard copy of each Prime-Alert issue alongwith the data on floppy.

**The other services available on floppies include:**

| | |
|---|---|
| Prime BB: | **A post-issue information package on public issues** |
| Prime WU-P & R: | **Weekly issue update service on Public & Rights Issues** |
| Prime-ADC: | **Addresses of companies who enter the capital market** |
| Prime TFB: | **Top 500 brokers floppy** |
| Prime IUN: | **Individual underwriting commission statement** |
| Prime-PMB: | **Primary market brokers database** |
| Right BB: | **A post-issue information package on rights issues** |

### 4.10 *ICRA Information Products (Investment Information & Credit Rating Agency)*

ICRA Limited (formerly, Investment Information and

Credit Rating Agency of India Limited) was established in 1991 as an independent and professional company providing investment information and credit rating services. As the growth and globalization of Indian capital markets have led to an exponential surge in demand for professional credit risk analysis, ICRA has actively responded to this need by executing assignments including credit ratings, equity grading and mandated studies spanning diverse industrial sectors. In addition to being India's leading credit rating agency with expertise in virtually every sector of the Indian economy, ICRA has broad-based its services to the corporate and financial sectors, both in India and overseas and presently offers its services under three heads, namely,

- Rating Services
- Advisory Services
- Information Services

Under its Information Services Division ICRA produces a number of Investment Information products on economy, business and industry and corporates. The details are as under:

4.10.1 *Economy*

4.10.1.1 *Money & Finance Bulletin* : The Money & Finance Bulletin is a quarterly publication directed towards individuals with an interest in understanding the reasons underlying policy initiatives and outcomes.

4.10.2 *Industry*

4.10.2.1 *Reports in The Industry Watch Series* : Reports in the Industry Watch Series present in-depth analyses on different industries, providing an insight into industry competitiveness, the imperatives for succeeding in a global scenario and the relative positions of industry participants. The reports present extensive information and in-depth analyses across a spectrum of industries. The following is the list of industries being tracked

- **Automobiles**

  Automobile Components

  Two/Three-Wheelers

  Tyres
- **Cement**
- **Consumer Durables**

  White Goods

  Consumer Electronics
- **Fast Moving Consumer Goods**

  Breweries & Distilleries

  Foods & Beverages
- **Fertilisers**
- **Hotels**
- **Media**

  Internet
- **Metals**

  Steel

  Aluminium
- **Oil & Gas**
- **Petrochemicals**

  Basic Petrochemicals

  Downstream Petrochemicals

  Polymers
- **Pharmaceuticals**
- **Telecommunication**

  Basic Telecom

  Value-Added Telecom Services

4.10.2.2 *Industry Comment* : Industry comment is a brief industry overview on the following industries:

- Aluminium
- Automotive Components

- Cement
- Consumer Products
- Cotton Yarn
- Fertilisers
- Hotels
- Oil & Gas
- Paints
- Paper
- Passenger Cars
- Pharmaceuticals
- Polyester
- Polymers
- Software
- Steel
- Telecommunication Cable
- Telecommunication Services
- Two Wheelers
- Tyres

4.10.3 *Corporate*

4.10.3.1 Corporate Reports : The reports provide exhaustive and reliable information on corporate entities besides analysis by our Research Analysts. The reports are designed to facilitate the investment/credit decisions of investors/lenders. The list of corporates being tracked is mentioned below:

1. Arvind Mills Limited
2. Ashima Syntex Limited
3. Asian Hotels Limited
4. Asian Paints Limited
5. Bajaj Auto Limited
6. Balaji Hotels & Enterprises Limited
7. Ballarpur Industries Limited

8. Bank of Baroda Limited
9. Bata India Limited
10. Bausch & Lomb India Limited
11. Bharat Petroleum Corporation Limited
12. Bishnauth Tea Company Limited
13. BPL Limited
14. Britannia Industries Limited
15. Cadbury India Limited
16. CMC Limited
17. Cochin Refineries Limited
18. Colgate-Palmolive (India) Limited
19. Corporation Bank Limited
20. Dabur India Limited
21. E I H Limited
22. Exide Industries Limited
23. F A G Precision Bearings Limited
24. Finolex Cables Limited
25. Gammon India Limited
26. Gas Authority of India Limited
27. Global Tele-Systems Limited
28. Godrej Soaps Limited
29. Goodricke Group Limited
30. Great Eastern Shipping Company Ltd
31. Gujarat Alkalies & Chemicals Limited
32. Gujarat Gas Limited
33. H D F C Bank Limited
34. HCL Infosystems Limited
35. Henkel Spic India Limited
36. Hero Honda Motors Limited
37. Hindalco Industries Limited
38. Hindustan Lever Limited
39. Hindustan Petroleum Corporation Ltd

40. Housing Development Fin Corpn Ltd
41. I T C Bhadrachalam Paperboards Ltd
42. Indian Aluminium Company Limited
43. Indian Hotels Company Limited
44. Indian Oil Corporation Limited
45. Indian Petrochemicals Corpn Limited
46. Indian Rayon & Industries Limited
47. Infosys Technologies Limited
48. Ircon International Limited
49. ITC Agrotech Limited
50. ITC Hotels Limited
51. ITC Limited
52. Jagatjit Industries Limited
53. Jindal Iron & Steel Company Ltd
54. Jindal Polyester Limited
55. Jumbo Bags Limited
56. Kinetic Engineering Limited
57. Kinetic Honda Limited
58. L M L Limited
59. Larsen & Toubro Limited
60. M R F Limited
61. Madras Refineries Limited
62. Madura Coats Limited
63. Mahanagar Telephone Nigam Ltd
64. Mahavir Spinning Mills Limited
65. Mangalore Refinery & Petrochem Ltd
66. Marico Industries Limited
67. Morepen Laboratories Ltd
68. National Aluminium Company Limited
69. Nestle India Limited
70. Nicholas Piramal India Limited
71. Nirma Limited

72. Parasrampuria Synthetics Limited
73. Pentafour Software & Exports Limited
74. Procter & Gamble India Limited
75. Punjab Anand Lamps Limited
76. Punjab Tractors Limited
77. Ranbaxy Laboratories Limited
78. Raymond Limited
79. Reckitt & Colman Of India Ltd.
80. Reliance Industries Limited
81. Reliance Petroleum Limited
82. S K F Bearings India Limited
83. Satyam Computer Services Limited
84. Seshasayee Paper Mills Limited
85. Shipping Corporation Of India Limited
86. SRF Limited
87. Steel Authority of India Limited
88. Sterlite Industries Limited
89. Subhash Projects & Marketing Limited
90. Tata Engineering & Locomot. Co Ltd
91. Tata Iron & Steel Company Limited
92. Tata Tea Limited
93. Timken India Limited
94. Unitech Limited
95. United Breweries Limited
96. Vardhman Spinning and Gen Mills Ltd
97. Videocon International Limited
98. Videsh Sanchar Nigam Limited
99. Wipro Ltd.
100. Wockhardt Limited

4.10.3.2 *ICRA Corporate Review* : The ICRA Corporate Review (ICR) provides select information and insightful commentary on a universe of Indian corporates. It is designed with the specific objective of providing timely access to independent, unbiased and dependable opinions on Indian companies. At present it covers about 300 companies. Besides the online version, ICRA also has the CD-ROM edition.

4.10.4 *Others*

4.10.4.1 *Rating Profile* : A unique bi-monthly source of reference from ICRA, the Rating Profile contains the rationales for the ratings assigned, and the rating symbols & implications.

4.10.4.2 *Rating Update* : A bi-monthly rating reference, the Rating Update serves as a single-point reference on all ICRA ratings outstanding.

4.10.4.3 *Press Releases* : (as and when issued): All press releases issued by ICRA, including releases pertaining to ratings assigned or revised. Press releases covering industry reports or outlook, and new services/products will also be provided to the subscribers.

**5. ICRA Interactive**

***www.icraindia.com***

The last three years have witnessed a significant development in web related technologies worldwide thus making it possible to capitalise on the web's potential to deliver increasing amounts of information to a burgeoning community of web users. As the web is rapidly transformed into a vast resource for meeting information requirements, it is imperative for corporates to formulate a serious web strategy as part of their overall growth plan.

Icraindia.com was originally set up in 1997 through a host based in Michigan, USA. The objective was that of reaching out to the business community worldwide in order to create awareness about ICRA and its range of investment related services and products in India.

- Free Areas

All users may access information from the following areas freely.

Ratings Outstanding

Business Briefings

Rating Actions

Free samples of ICR, Corporate Reports, Industry Comment

Money & Finance Abstracts

All visitors have free access to online features like **Search and E-mail Updates (including customised updates)**

**6. Freely Available Resources**

Over the last decade all aspects of computer technology, processing techniques, storage media and input/output devices have become faster, more compact, sophisticated and less expensive. Internet is one of the boons of information technology. Introduction of Internet and web technology has reduced the cost, time and manpower of publishing documents. As a result organizations, institutions and even individuals are publishing on the Internet.

The place of exploitation of Internet by the Library and information center are unlimited and endless. Internet provides a wealth of information such as online E-books, E-journals, E-news letter, E-database etc. These vast resources can be accessed by the library and information centers and can be provided to the users Online information sources are referred to be free when access to the sources are not dependent on subscription or membership in an organization or a publisher. Among the freely accessible digital information resources identified at URL http://www.geocities.com/bhavinajin , following are most important ones:

### 6.1 *Electronics Books (http:/ / www.geocities.com/ bhavinaj/ EC_Books. html)*

Several projects like project Gutenberg for e-books and digital library project like University of Pennsylvania, University of Virginia E-Book Library have been undertaken which also include Social Science and related discipline. Important e-book sites are described below

#### 6.1.1 *Gutenberg Project on electronic books online (http:/ / www.promo.net/ pg)*

Thousands of e-books are available in this site free of charge. The site is having browsing facility by Author, and by Title. It also provides advanced search facility by Author or by Title (words). Author wise list of e-books is available at http://www.promo.net/pg/authors.zip and Title wise list of e-books is available at http://www.promo.net/pg/titles.zip and current list of e-books is available as GUTINDEXALL at the FTP site at the University of North Carolina ftp://ibiblio.org/pub/docs/books/gutenberg/GUTINDEXALL

#### 6.1.2 *University of Pennsylvania online book page*

The Online Books Page is a website that facilitates access to books that are freely readable over the Internet. This site includes the different sections like Books Online, News, Features, Archives. The Online Books Page was founded and is edited by John Mark Ockerbloom. He is a digital library planner and researcher at the University of Pennsylvania. The online books listed on this page have been authored, placed online, and hosted by a wide variety of individuals and groups throughout the world. The local index of this page includes more than 15,000 English works in various formats. All are free for personal, non-commercial use. Near about 585 number of books on Social Science and 795 number of books on other interdisciplinary subjects.

6.1.3 *Electronic Text Centre of Virginia University*

Near about 141 numbers of books on following topics are available in the Electronic Text Center of the Virginia University.

6.1.4 *Bartleby Books online (http://www.Bartleby.com)*

The Bartleby is one of the Internet publishers of literature and reference providing students, researchers and intellectually curious with unlimited access to books and information on the web, free of charge. The following reference books are freely available Online's from Bartleby Books online.

1. Columbia Encyclopedia, 6th ed :- http://www.bartleby.com/65/
2. Columbia Encyclopedia, 6th ed: Index to biographical entries:- http://www.bartleby.com/65/a0.html
3. Anatomy of the Human Body :- http://www.bartleby.com/107/
4. Columbia Gazetteer of North America , Edited by Saul B. Cohen :- http://www.bartleby.com/69/
5. World Fact book 2001:- http://www.bartleby.com/151/
6. Columbia World of Quotations, Edited by Robert Andrews, Mary Biggs and Michael Seidel :- http://www.bartleby.com/66/
7. Roget's II : The New Thesaurus, 3rd ed:- http://www.bartleby.com/62/
8. American Heritage Dictionary of the English Language:- http://www.bartleby.com/61/
9. Encyclopedia of World History : Ancient, Medieval and Modern :- http://www.bartleby.com/67/

**6.2 *Electronic Journals***
***(http:// www.geocities.com/ bhavinajin/ journal.html***

Near about 36 online electronic journals on Social

Science and related discipline freely available are identified so far. Most of the journals are available in full text. Some journals are restricted and only abstracts of those journals are freely accessible

**6.3 *Databases***

6.3.1 *(http://www.geocities.com/bhavinajin/databases.html)*

Databases which are available free of charges are identified and linked in this section. Out of them followings are most important ones.

6.3.2 *Social Science Gateway (http://sosig.ac.uk/*

The Social Science Information Gateway (SOSIG) is a freely available Internet service which aims to provide a trusted source of selected, high quality Internet information for students, academics, researchers and practitioners in the social sciences, business and law. It is part of the UK Resource Discovery Network.

6.3.3 *Social Science Search Engine (http://sosig.ac.uk/harvester.html)*

This is a database of over 50,000 Social Science Web pages. Whereas the resources found in the SOSIG Internet Catalogue have been selected by subject experts, those in the Social Science Search Engine have been collected by software called a 'harvester' (similar mechanisms may be referred to as 'robots' or 'Web crawlers'). All the pages collected from the main Internet catalogue which provides the equivalent of a social science search engine. It provides both simple and advanced search facilities.

6.3.4 *Ingenta Database (http://www.ingenta.com/)*

This database was formerly known as Uncover Database (http://uncweb.carl.org) and recently it has been taken over by Ingenta integrated to Ingenta's full text delivery service. The contents and abstracts are available free of charges. It contains 13,721,653 articles and 27,444 publications and covers different subject areas including Social Sciences. Ingenta now offers individuals the ability to sign up for email Table of Contents (TOC) alerts, which run exclusively from 5,400 full-text electronic journals. Individuals may sign up for alerts from up to five journals. Institutions and corporations interested in offering this service to their patrons can now buy a site license for unlimited TOC and Search Alerts

6.3.5 *ERIC Database ( http://ericir.sys.edu/Eric )*

This database is produced with Public funding by the U.S. Department of Education. Citations found in the Database are therefore public domain and may be freely copied and redistributed. This includes posting citations on Web sites created by individuals or agencies. The Document citations represent papers, reports, government documents and other materials published outside of the journal environment. The database provides both Simple and Advanced Search facilities.

**7. Libraries-Virtual Libraries-Digital Libraries**

**7.1** ***(http:// www.geocities.com/ bhavinajin/ lib.html )***

In this section reputed libraries all over the world, different digital libraries and virtual libraries are linked. Among all the libraries followings are the most important ones.

**7.2** ***World Libraries on the World Wide Web (http:// www.123world.com/ libraries/ index.html#t)***

It provides ultimate source of authentic and reliable information about 137 numbers of libraries of the world including Social Science on the net. This list of libraries includes the link of public libraries, research libraries, state libraries, national archives, libraries of different educational institutions, agricultural and technical libraries, business libraries, science libraries, and IMF libraries all over the world. It is arranged in alphabetical order.

### 7.3 *Digital Library: University of California : ( http:// elib.cs.berkeley.edu )*

The University of California, Berkeley Digital Library Project is a part of Digital Libraries initiative, sponsored by the National Science Foundation and many others. It provides quick access of the collection, overview of the collection, image retrieval by image content, document image analysis and distributed search.

### 7.4 *Social Science Virtual Library (http:// vlib Social Sciences.html)*

*Digital Resources in Social Sciences*

Social Sciencesinclude the following disciplines : cultural (or social) anthropology, sociology, social psychology, political science and economics'. 'Also included are social and economic geography and those areas of education that deal with the social contexts of learning and the relation of the school of the social order. History is regarded by many as a social science, and certain areas of historical study are almost indistinguishable from work done in the social sciences.

covers sociology, political science, economics and business, commerce, public administration, anthropology, education and law. In India library and Information Science subject is also covered in the social sciences faculty.

## 8. On Line Journals

India approximately publishes 12,000 journals out of which about 1300 belong to social sciences. Most of the journals published in regional languages are not covered in Ulrich's Periodical directory. In comparison to India on International scene about 50,000 journals are published in social sciences whereas in science more than one lakh journals are published world over. Standard journals published in U.S.A. and European countries have their web sites and most of them are available on online as well as in print form.

So far Indian journals are concerned most of these are in print form. Almost all the standard and institutional journals have their web sites. Some web sites have detailed information with home page facility. No Indian periodical directory indicates which periodicals are on on-line or on CD ROM. Complete Indian Journal on online is a rarity.

**9. Reference Databases**

Reference databases contain representations of original sources of data, information or knowledge. They refer the searcher to more complete printed information sources. Records in reference database are distillations created through the analytical processes of cataloguing, indexing, abstracting and classification. Reference databases are intended to serve information retrieval functions.

**10. Bibliographic Databases**

Undoubtedly most of the bibliographic databases provide references to journals articles in areas of science and technology, and to a lesser extent in disciplines of the social sciences and humanities. There are databases like: **U.S. Exports, Full Text Databases** : original textual material belonging to primary source items, such as encyclopaedia, court decision, newspaper, or journal articles. Examples are **Academic American Encyclopedia,** it consists of 32,000 general encyclopedia articles.

**11. Chronolog News Letter**

It is produced by DIALOG Information Retrieval Service. The online version of the monthly news publication of DIALOG 1981 to present.

**12. Historical Abstracts**

Important works of American and European History are covered is this abstract. Brief description of each work has been covered. However, publications of Asian and African countries find no significant place in this source.

## 13. CD ROM Databases

It is a fact that research is very fast in science, engineering, medicine, technology and particularly computer technology, research of course is going on in the social sciences however, it cannot be compared with research development in science and technology. Some important CD ROM databases in social sciences have been briefly described. Almost all of these belong to advanced countries.

### 13.1 *Ulrich's on CD ROM*

It is very useful database for complete bibliographical detail of periodicals. It is an international source covering periodicals of all the countries numbering about 2,30,000.

### 13.2 *Lisa Plus on CD ROM*

It provides abstracts from over 550 periodicals from more than 68 countries along with unpublished academic and institutional research from the current research in library and information science. LISA plus includes US-State library journals and new titles in information technology. Unrivaled international coverage, no competitor can match the world wide coverage of LISA PLUS, with 150 non-English language journals from 68 countries in 35 languages.

### 13.3 *Bowker/ Whiteaker : Global Books in Print on CD ROM*

This source gives the most authoritative coverage of English language titles worldwide. Information specialists and booksellers will be able to locate, access and other material published in English throughout the world.

### 13.4 *Books in Print on CD-ROM*

It is a classic bibliographic database for all current and forthcoming American titles in print. Coverage of the titles is about 1.6 million entries. Books in Print with book reviews offers all the benefits and features of complete books in print database, combined with tens of thousands of unabridged book reviews from 14 of the most esteemed book reviewing media. This two disc product includes bibliography and ordering information on 2.5 million bindings including books, audio-books and videos, either in print or out of print.

### 13.5 *Assia Plus on CD ROM*

Applied Social Sciences index and Abstracts data base is a unique subject coverage. It has an international scope, ASSIA PLUS covers publication from over 16 countries. It is complete social science tool for both practical and academic disciplines.

### 13.6 *Bhi Plus on CD ROM*

British Humanities Index is an indispensable part of any current humanities serials collection as well as historical reference. An ideal starting point for any research work, the BHI PLUS CD ROM gives instant and flexible access to the British humanities index records from 1985 to the present, over 217000 entries.

### 13.7 *Institute of Management International Database Plus on CD ROM*

It is a complete management tool for the students of management, business schools, academic libraries and personnel/training departments in companies professional institutes and consultancies. It consists of 35,000 Abstracts 25,000 books, working pages, audio-video material etc.

### 13.8 *Envorpment Abstracts on CD ROM*

It gives comprehensive and effective access to over 2,30,000 citations from 1971 to date.

### 13.9 *World Guide to Libraries Plus on CD ROM*

A single CD-ROM which is an invaluable research and contact source. Fast retrieval of the information you need on worldwide libraries and with the combinable search criteria you can search for libraries with certain special collections.

### 13.10 *American Library Directory on CD-ROM*

This powerful new product will help you find your way through the vast US book trade and library communities. It has information about 39000 libraries and retail and antiquarian book dealers. UNESCO launches information compact disc. It has information about UNESCO's publications, education, educational innovation and literacy. OCLC computer library database on CD ROM is the second of four databases in the OCLC library series available from silver platter and OCLC online union catalogue, a database of over 24 million records controlled by over 5000 members libraries throughout the world. The OCLC computer library is an international bibliography of computer and communication materials coverage span the 20th century and includes more than 2,70,000 records published on the disc, the OCLC computer library database is updated annually.

### 13.11 *BNB on CD ROM*

The British National Bibliography (BNB) is also available on CDROM as two distinct products. Records of 1960-85 are contained on two discs and current discs (updated and produced quarterly) contains records from 1986 onwards.

### 13.12 *PAIS on CD ROM*

Public Affairs information service, inc. brings out PAIS on CD ROM covering over 2,50,000 records beginning in 1972 and indexes worldwide information on public affairs from a variety of sources.

### 13.13 *Index Translationum on CD ROM*

It covers about 60,000 works translated and published since 1979 in more than 100 countries of the world.

### 13.14 *Reference/ Sources on CD-ROM*

CD-ROM offers excellent media for covering reference sources. Grolier was the first publisher to use optical media to provide access to its Academic American Encyclopedia. The CD ROM version, called Electronic Encyclopaedia has sophisticated searching capabilities. The first British Encyclopaedia recorded on CD ROM is the 8th edition of Hutchinson Encyclopaedia, McGraw-Hill Encyclopaedia of science and technology. Pergamon international Encyclopaedia of Education, New Encyclopaedia Britannica, Oxford English Dictionary, Guinness disc of records are some very important reference sources available on CD ROM. Microsoft book-shelf, a library of ten references works stored on a single CD ROM disc is perhaps the best selling CD ROM service. Gale directory of databases 1995 lists 4420 databases available on CD ROM. During the next six years large number of reference sources are now on CD ROM.

### 13.15 *Serial's Directory*

It is a CD ROM version of EBSIO's serials directory covering 1,13,000 serial publications including annuals, irregulars and ceased titles.

### 13.16 *Dissertation Abstracts*

Dissertation Abstracts Humanities and Social Sciences is a comprehensive source of dissertation information covering from 1861 to present. It covers Doctoral dissertations and master theses, representing work over 1000 universities throughout the world, but mainly North American graduate school and many European Universities. The database includes abstracts from 1980 forwards master theses. Abstracts are written by the author of the dissertation/theses and average 350 words and 150 words in length respectively. This database is brought out by UMI.USA with quarterly updates covering various subjects such as education, business and economics, history sociology, language and literature, law, political science, music, fine arts, arts, cinema, philosophy, religion, theology and psychology. INFLIBNET centre has this database update.

### 13.17 *Econlit*

It is a fundamental research tool in economics. The database covers the international literature in economics, since 1969 and provides bibliographic citations with selected abstracts of journal articles, books, dissertations and working papers, as well as articles in collective works such as conference proceedings, collected essay volumes and full text book reviews. It has over 3,97,000 records covering the topics economic development, forecasting and history, fiscal and monetary theory, business and public finance, international, healthcare religion-urban economics etc.

### 13.18 *PSYCLIT : Psychological Literature*

This CD ROM database is published by the American Psychological association, covers publications in the fields of Psychology and behaviour including such subject areas as social, clinical, cognitive, developmental and education psychology and neuropsychological. Covering from 1974 through the present, it includes references and abstracts for articles from journals, and also for book chapters and books from 1987 to the present. This database is available with the INFLIBNET upto 1996.

### 13.19 *SSCI : Social Science Citation Index*

This is a multidisciplinary database with abstracts to the journal literature of the social sciences. It includes items relevant to the social science from the 7000 journals. Covered in the multidisciplinary ISI database. It includes author subject index, search by cited author, cited patents or cited papers. This database covers the literature on different subjects viz. education, business and economics, history, sociology, language, literature, law, political science, music, fine arts, arts, cinema, philosophy, religion, theology and psychology. It is brought out by institute of scientific information, U.S.A. and is available with the INFLIBNET for the period 1995-96.

### 13.20 *SOCIOFILE : Sociological Abstracts*

Sociofile is a CD-ROM based fundamental tool for access to the latest international findings in theoretical and applied sociology, social science and political science. It contains abstracts from 2300 journals published since 1974 and enhanced bibliographic citations for dissertations added since 1986. The database combines sociological abstracts with social planning policy and development abstract (SOPODA). Sociofile covers journals articles, dissertations, book abstracts, chapter abstracts and association paper abstracts as well as form books, films and software etc. INFLIBNET centre has this database.

E-journals available through internet applications. LIBRES Library and Information Science Research Electronic Journal, Mc Journal : The journal of Academic media Librarianship, PACS review, and The Oliver Tree : A library and information Science Electronic Journal exemplify this type of electronic journal. Now these titles are available on Web. Subscriptions and access to this category of electronic journal are free. Although there are a number of benefits yet its credibility is yet to be seen in future.

Some major e-journals provides are American Chemical Society (http://pubs.acs.org) Academic Press:/IDEAL LIBRARY (http://www.ideallibrary. com) Cambridge University Press (http.//journals.cup.org) Elsevier: Science Direct (http://www.sciencedirect.com) Highwire Press (http://www .highwire.org) Kluwer Online journals (http://kapis.www.wkap.nl/kaphtml.htm

## 14. J-Gate

J-Gate is an Internet gateway and portal set up nearly two-years ago by Informatics (India) Ltd Bangalore. It offers affordable access to global electronic journal literature. It provides seamless access to journal articles through their massive database interface of 8,500+ e-journals.

### 14.1 *J-Gate Features and Benefits*

- Link to full text are provided from TOC and database interfaces for every article
- Weekly content updating.
- Author email address where available.
- Searchable database by Author, Title word, and subject-words.
- Basic Search module.
- Advanced Search module.
- Author Abstracts where available.
- Every journal is classified at three levels of hierarchical classification.
- Password Management System
- Common customized interface for e-journal consortia of specific client groups.
- Facility to monitor the usage by publishers and libraries
- My TOC - Individual users can create their own TOC service for journals of their choice

### 14.2 *J-Gate Products and Services*

14.2.1 *J-Gate TOC (Table of Contents)*

- 8500+ e-Journals (as of November 2002).
- Journals on by Journal title, title word, subject categories and year of publication.
- TOC for all journals in an uniform browsable format.
- Basic bibliographic data with abstract (where available).
- Author Address and email where available.

- Link to full-text.
- Link to Union catalog for finding availability.
- Weekly updating.
- Access by Internet.

### 14.3 *J-Gate Database*

- All Journal articles listed in TOC are compiled into Database.
- Classification by two levels of subject category.
- Subject indexing.
- Search by title word, author, subject keywords, year and any combination.
- Basic bibliographic data with abstract (where available).
- Author Address and email where available.
- Link to full-text.
- Link to Union catalog for finding availability (under development).
- Weekly updating with progressive accumulation.
- Access by Internet.

### 14.4 *J-Gate Customer Content (JCC)*

- A local intranet solution.
- TOC and Database services customized to all journals "subscribed" by XLRI Jamshedpur.
- Customized J-Gate Software installed at XLRI-Jamshedpur premises.
- Weekly delivery of TOC and Database Content.

### 14.5 *JCC for Consortia ( JCC)*

- JCC service for a homogeneous group of clients.
- JCC software is installed in each client site.
- Common TOC and Database services for journals subscribed by all the clients forming consortium. Content is mirrored in each participating library.
- Link to union catalog for resource sharing. Email request

for article photocopies can be sent directly by users while browsing articles/abstracts, to any chosen library.

### 14.6 *J-gate Infrastructure*

- 7-days/24 hours access.
- High-speed in-house internet infrastructure.
- Automated content capturing and conversion system ensuring high quality content aggregation.
- In-house software development team.
- Safe and reliable high-capacity storage system for content storage.
- Data-refreshing system for maintaining the content for all time against technological obsolesce.

## 15. Online Database Sources and Services on Engineering

Following are some of the important websites meant for engineering information users. They are the main links which will lead to many sub links in the form of collection of the home pages, related links, databases and other electronic resources covering a wide spectrum of engineering information.

### 15.1 *Engineering E-Library, Sweden (EELS) http://www.eels.lub.lu.se/*

The Engineering E-Library, Sweden (EELS) is an information system for quality assessed information resources on the Internet. EELS are an attempt to provide mainly the technical universities with links to evaluated resources. EELS is a cooperative project of the Swedish Universities of Technology Libraries.

Almost all of the selected EELS resources are free of charge and no special conditions for accessing them exist. However, for most subject fields within engineering there are also very important databases distributed through Internet but not free of charge. Passwords are needed to use these databases and they can be reached through other networks as well. The reason for including them is to emphasize their importance in subject orientated information searching. The coverage will vary from subject field to subject field during the first period of EELS.

### 15.2 *EEVL http:/ / www.eevl.ac.uk/*

EEVL is the Internet Guide to Engineering, Mathematics and Computing. EEVL's mission is to provide access to quality networked engineering, mathematics and computing resources, and be the national focal point for online access to information in these subjects. It is an award-winning free service, created and run by a team of information specialists from a number of universities and institutions in the UK.

EEVL's target audience is students, staff and researchers in higher and further education, as well as anyone else working, studying or looking for information in Engineering, Mathematics and Computing

### 15.3 *Australian Virtual Engineering Library (AVEL) http:/ / www.avel.edu.au/*

AVEL has been recently changed as the AVEL Sustainability Knowledge Network with a vision to create a web space that brings people and information together around the overlapping themes of engineering, new technologies and the imperatives of sustainability as it impacts on a diverse range of industry and community sectors.

### 15.4 *Avel Sustainability Knowledge Network*

AVEL Sustainability Knowledge Network is a portal and brokerage service for engineers, other professionals and researchers concerned with sustainable systems. It is also a resource for students in senior secondary and tertiary education.

Sustainability is used in the sense of the triple bottom line, i.e. financial (including technical), ecological and social sustainability. The products of engineering must not only be technically sound and cost effective, they must also be sustainable in both the ecological and social dimensions. This demands innovative solutions built on solid engineering foundations, drawing on emerging technologies and incorporating ecological and societal considerations systemically.

The concept is to create a web-place - a Sustainability Knowledge Network - that brings people and information together around the overlapping themes of engineering, new technologies and the imperatives of sustainability as it impacts a diverse range of industry and community sectors. The goal is to evolve the Network into a semantic web that supports research, practice and e-learning as the web tools allow.

By creating the Sustainability Knowledge Network, the AVEL team is leading the development of a global network called the Virtual Environmental and Sustainable Systems Engineering Library or VESSEL. The International Council for Engineering and Technology (ICET) initiated the VESSEL project.

The Sustainability Knowledge Network is the logical development of the award winning Australasian Virtual Engineering Library (AVEL). AVEL is a gateway of quality web resources developed collaborativelyby a national team through an Australian Research Council (ARC) Research Infrastructure Grant from 1998-2002.

### 15.4.1 *Avel - Virtual Environment and Sustainable Systems Engineering Library (Vessel)*

VESSEL is the name of the World Virtual Engineering Library Network which is being established by the International Council for Engineering and Technology (ICET) with the support of the United Nations Educational, Scientific and Cultural Organization (UNESCO).

The principal emphasis of the VESSEL network will be to provide developing nations with improved access to resources that can assist in education in science, technology and engineering, at senior levels in schools and technical colleges and universities. The network will aim particularly to provide resources to teachers and lecturers, and will seek to meet the requirements identified within the developing countries.

Australian Virtual Engineering Library (AVEL) is the lead library for the VESSEL network. With the support of the Institution of Engineers, Australia (IEAust) and the Institution of Professional Engineers, New Zealand (IPENZ), we are currently building up a substantial virtual engineering library.

### 15.5 *Elsevier Engineering Information (Ei) http://www.ei.org*

Engineering Information Inc has an important role in the engineering community. For the universities, Ei products and services provide both faculty and students the most current information available anywhere. In addition, Ei educates students in the use of formal information tools. For those in the corporate community, Ei has been able to provide timely information to facilitate innovation, deliver critical competitive information and directly contribute to the enhancement of product design.

In 1998 Elsevier Science, the world's largest publisher of scientific, technical , technical and medical publications, acquired Ei. Ei's headquarters are based at the Stevens Institute Campus in the town of Hoboken, New Jersey, USA. Ei also has offices in the United Kingdom and Japan.

Engineering Information Inc. is the leader in providing online information, knowledge and support of the highest professional relevance for research and industrial practitioners in applied physical sciences and engineering. Their mission since 1884 has been to keep our customers competitive with our up-to-date research and information services. They are working to fulfill their mission primarily through the creation of timesaving, cost-effective and efficient products.

The history of their products have spans over a century's worth of time. The founder member Dr. John Butler Johnson first published Index Notes, in 1884. The first resource of its kind, Index Notes only articles of permanent value, providing a concise description that allowed the reader to determine its importance. Now in the 21st century Ei products have taken advantage of the electronic information age by enabling its customers to reach millions of pieces of information in one step. The following section presents details about each of the above services of Ei.

Engineering Information (Ei) offers an array of products and services for universities, corporations and government organizations. Products include:

15.5.1 *Engineering Village 2*™

A desktop information delivery system that provides access to multiple databases via one interface

15.5.2 *Chem Village*™

Provides access to multiple chemistry databases via a single interface. Research bibliographic, news, patent and handbook databases through a single point of entry.

15.5.3 *Paper Village 2*™

Electronic information service for the Paper & Pulp Industry

15.5.4 *Compendex*®

A comprehensive interdisciplinary engineering database with over six million summaries of journal articles, technical reports, and conference papers and proceedings in electronic form, dating from 1970 forward

15.5.5 *PaperChem*™

Comprehensive bibliographic database that covers international journal literature related to the pulp and paper industry

15.5.6 *EnCompass*™

An electronic database that provides timely technical literature and patent information for the petroleum, petrochemical, natural gas and energy industries.

15.5.7 *The Engineering Index*

An organized compilation of bibliographic citations and abstracts covering the world's technological literature in all disciplines

15.5.8 *Abstract Bulletin of Paper Science and Technology*

Crucial coverage for the pulp and paper community, this important resource contains hundreds of records each month

15.5.9 *Chemical Business NewsBase*

A leading database of worldwide chemical business news and information

## 15.6 *Engineering Village*

It is a powerful way to search across multiple databases via one interface. In just a few seconds even the first time user can reach over 6,000,000 summaries of journal articles, technical reports, and conference papers and proceedings dating from 1970 forward as well as more than 10,000 website abstracts, and 80 full-text searchable handbooks, patents and standards.

- Links to full-text articles from Elsevier Science, the Institute of Physics, the American Institute of Physics (including the American Society of Civil Engineers and the American Society of Mechanical Engineers), Springer-Verlag, John Wiley & Sons and Academic Press.

- Ability to order individual documents from the Linda Hall Library
- Fully customized features
- Two levels of search capabilities: Quick search and Expert Search.

**Multiple Databases to choose from:**

15.6.1 *Ei Compendex®*

The most comprehensive interdisciplinary engineering database in the world:

- Over 6,000,000 records from 1969 to the present 250,000 records added annually
- Updated every seven days
- References and abstracts from over 5,000 journals, conferences and reports

15.6.2 *United State Patent and Trademark Office*

- Existing Patents and Trademarks dating from 1976
- Access to the Patent and Trademark Depository Libraries
- How to apply for a patent
- Register practitioners registered to practice before the PTO

15.6.3 *CRC Press*

One of the world's leading publishers of engineering handbooks:

- On-line access via ENGnetBASE
- Over 80 engineering handbooks on-line and full text searchable *Additional subscription fee required for handbook access

15.6.4 *Industry Specs and Standards:*

Comprehensive collection of industry standards and specifications

- Over 20,000 abstracts available with links to full text articles *Initial fees required for full standards

15.6.5 *Website Abstracts:*

- Access to more than 10,000 website abstracts
- Consistent search results ensured via the Ei Thesaurus
- Websites evaluated based on research value, technical content and relevant information

Abstracts ranked based on content, ease-of-use, presentation, and organization of information

### 15.7 *Chem Village*

It is a new resource that provides a 'first stop shop' for scientists and professionals in the chemical industry.

The features of ChemVillage include

Three Databases:

- Chimica
- Chemical Business NewsBase
- Beilstein Abstracts

**Other features include:**

- Links to full text articles in online journals
- Search assistance using Reference Services and Ask a Chemist
- Unlimited usage for one annual subscription fee

## 16. Encompass

With access to over 1.5 million selections, the EnCompass® database is the premier international information source for the petroleum, petrochemical, natural gas and energy industries.

Providing timely as well as technical literature dating from 1964, EnCompass™ provides historical technical literature, patent information, technology applications, and business news and market intelligence. All information is easily found because of precision searching based on a controlled vocabulary.

- EnCompassLit™ is the technical literature database focusing on worldwide petroleum-related materials. Records are derived from trade and scientific journals, conference proceedings, and technical reports with original abstracts plus abstracts from other important sources.
- EnCompassPat™ is the patent database covering patents from nearly 40 countries. It contains EnCompass world-renowned value-added indexing, which is designed to allow researchers to locate all relevant patents with ease and confidence. It includes special features not available elsewhere, such as roles and links.

**Available Databases**

**16.1 *PaperChem*™**

A comprehensive bibliographic database covering international journal literature related to pulp and paper technology. Includes abstracts of journal articles, conference papers and technical reports with more than 480,000 records covering:

- Forestry
- Hemicelluloses
- Carbohydrates
- The Chemistry of Cellulose
- Lignin and Extractives
- Engineering and Process Control
- Corrugated and Particle Board
- Corrosion
- Equipment

- Packaging
- Pollution
- Water & Power

### 16.2 *Website Abstracts:*

Over 3,000 websites selected and reviewed by industry experts based on their research value, technical content and relevant information

### 16.3 *US Patent Office and Trademark Office:*

- Over 6,000,000 patents dating from 1976
- Access to the Patent and Trademark Depository Libraries
- How to apply for a patent

### 16.4 *Paper Village*

It is the electronic information service for the paper and pulp industry professional in engineering, research and development and management.

Designed to find informed answers quickly, the PaperVillage2™ provides access to a series of databases and multiple websites.

## 17. E4 Engineering :www.e4 engineering.com

The e4 network is a group of sites from UK business publisher centaur communication dedicated providing information and services to those working in industry and the engineering professions. The first two sites in the e4 network ,e4 engineering.com and e4 data.com, our job site e4 jobnet.com and directory site subcontract services, e4 subcontracting.com E4 engineering.com is a First European portal site, brings content from centaurs market leading engineering magazines along with news and features updated.

E4 data.com is a subscription based service- data is the place to look for technical specification and data sheets.

E4 jobnet.com is a specialists recruitment site for engineering industries at regular intervals throughout the week updation.

E4 subcontracting.com is a directory of subcontracting services easy searches by company, service, location or by quality approval.

**18. INFOMINE: http:/ / www.infomine.com**

INFOMINE is a virtual library of Internet resources relevant to faculty, students, and research staff at the university level. It contains useful Internet resources such as databases, electronic journals, electronic books, bulletin boards, mailing lists, online library card catalogs, articles, directories of researchers, and many other types of information.

INFOMINE is librarian built. Librarians from The University of California, Wake Forest University, California State University, The University of Detroit - Mercy, and other universities and colleges have contributed to building INFOMINE.This web site is designed to work with any web browser that has the ability to display HTML and forms. Some JavaScript is used, but it is not necessary.

**19. Online Ethics Center for Engineering and Science: http:/ / www.onlineethics.org/**

The Online Ethics Center for Engineering and Science has been launched with a mission to provide engineers, scientists, and science and engineering students with resources for understanding and addressing ethically significant problems that arise in their work, and to serve those who are promoting learning and advancing the understanding of responsible research and practice in science and engineering.

**20. Bubl Link : http:/ / www.bubl.ac.uk**

Bubl is the name of a catalogue of selected Internet

resources covering all academic subject areas and catalogued according to DDC (Dewey Decimal Classification). All items are selected, evaluated, catalogued and described. Links are checked and fixed each month. LINK stands for Libraries of Networked Knowledge.

BUBL 5:15 provides an alternative interface to this catalogue, based on subject terms rather than DDC. The aim is to guarantee at least 5 relevant resources for every subject included, and a maximum of 15 resources for most subjects, hence the name 5:15. Big subject areas are broken down into smaller categories. However, the upper limit of 15 is not rigidly applied, so there may be up to 35 items for some subjects.

The BUBL LINK catalogue currently holds over 11,000 resources. This is far smaller than the databases held by major search engines, but it can provide a more effective route to information for many subjects, across all disciplines.

**21. Engnetbase : http:// www.engnet.com**

Database of engineering information providing access to data, facts, figures, graphs, equations, illustrations and charts. Information in the database is critically evaluated by prominent authors in the field. Disciplines covered include General Engineering, Structural Engineering, Communications, Electrical Engineering and Digital Signal Processing. The service is subscription-based, with a short free trial available. Auther of the site is Chapman and Hall.

**22. ERA Technology Conferences and Courses http:// www.era.com**

Diary of technical conferences, exhibitions, training courses, and seminars which concern the impact of developments in technology, the practical application of technology in a market, and the legislation or knowledge of industry. Author or this site is ERA Technology subjects covered include engineering news, technology transfer

**23. Flow Simulation's Engineering Links: http:www.eng links.com/**

A list of links to engineering resources on the Internet, arranged by category of engineering. Includes links to resources on aerospace engineering, CAD, civil engineering, marine engineering, materials science, and mechanical engineering.

Libraries are found to be a major market for CD-ROM products and obline databases. Major and large databases like ERIC, NTIS, COMPEDEX, Applied Science & Technology Index are some of the CD-ROM databases on Engineering & Technology available from Silver Platter and H.W. Wilson, UMI etc.Many of these databases are procured by different university libraries And R&D institutes.But access to them is restricted.Only staff, faculty and students of these organisations can avail them.Subscribing these databases individually by single user is really expensive.Institutional membership through subscription is always advisable.

**Free Engineering Resources Available on Internet (http:/ / www.geocities.com/ ghosh_svrec/ ebook.html)**

Due to advancement of web technology different organizations and institutions like Virginia University, Pennsylvania University and other organizations have taken up digital library and E-book projects. As a result different E-books are freely available online. Freely available online electronic books on Applied Science and Technology are identified and linked in this section. Near about 1067 number of E-books on Applied Science and Technology as stated below are freely accessible online.

**24. Online Electronic Journals**

**24.1 *(http:/ / www.geocities.com/ ghosh_svrec/ ejnl.html)***

About 104 number of journals on Applied Science and

Technology including Information Technology and Internet those are freely accessible are identified and linked with the above mentioned URL. Out of 104 journals 71 journals are available in full text and abstracts/contents of the remaining journals are also available free of charges. The number of journals is not exhaustive as the work is going on and it is a continuous process.

### 24.2 *Online Database (http:/ / www.geocities.com/ ghosh_svrec/ dbase. html)*

Different databases on Applied Science and Technology like Compendex, INSPEC, ASTP etc are available on CDROM as well as online, but it is not possible to subscribe the same for small and medium sized libraries and self financed Engineering colleges due to high rate of subscription. Near about 29 numbers of Online Databases which are freely accessible through Internet are identified and linked with URL http://www.geocities.com/ghosh_svrec/dbase.html. Out of 29 databases followings are the most important for the students and faculties of Applied Science and Technology.

### 24.3 *Earthquake Engineering Abstracts (http:/ / nisee.berkeley.edu/ eea.html)*

This database is maintained by the National Information Service for Earthquake Engineering (NIESEE), University of California, Barkeley. It covers the world's technical literature in earthquake engineering since 1971. Coverage includes technical reports, conference papers, monographs, journal articles. Provides Query by author, title, keywords, date. View citations and abstracts. It contains 10,00,000 records and is updated continuously. A maximum of 200 records will be displayed at a time. It provides author, title and keyword search and Boolean search under author, title and keywords and searchable in any range of year from 1971.

If the user click on the required article the abstract will be displayed on the screen as shown in figure no. 3 and the user can download or can take printout of the same. Materials in EEA are available on loan from the Earthquake Engineering Library at the University of California, Berkeley. More information will be available from EERC Library, 1301 S. 46th Street Richmond, CA 94804-4698, Phone: 510-231-9403, Fax: 510-231-9461 Email: eerclib@nisee.berkeley.edu

### 24.4 *U.S. Patent Full-Text and Full Image Database (http:/ / uspto.gov.patft)*

This database contains two parts i.e. (1) Patent Grants Database and (2) Patent Applications Database. Patent Grants Database includes full-text since 1976 and full-images since 1790. Patent Application Database is being published since 15th March, 2001. The databases are having following searching facilities:

- Quick search
- Advanced Search
- Patent number search (In case of Patent Grant Database)
- Application Number Search ( In case of Patent application Database)

It also provides Boolean search facilities and the database may also be searched by type and year. The search was conducted under term (1) "Digital signal" and (2) "processing" and option of year was "1996-2002". It retrieved 33013 number of documents. If the user click on the particular document the full text of the document along with abstract will be displayed and the user can download or get printout of the same.

### 24.5 *NASA Technical Reports Server (http:// techreports.larc.gov/ cgi-bin/ NTRS)*

The NASA Technical Report Server is an experimental

service that allows users to search the many different abstract and technical report servers maintained by various NASA centers and programs. Specifically, it is a unified interface to many separate WAIS servers. NTRS is both a superset of the of the various servers, and a canonical listing of the servers. It includes following databases:

| | |
|---|---|
| Ames Research Centre | NACA Reports (Abstracts only) |
| Astronomy & Astrophysics (ADS) | NACA Reports (Full text) |
| Dryden Flight Research Centre Glenn Research Centre | Physics and Geophysics (ADS) |
| Goddard Institute for Space Studies | CASITRS (RECONselect) |
| ICASE | Space Instrumentation (ADS) |
| Jet Propulsion Laboratory | Stennis Space Centre |
| Johnson Space Centre | LANL Astrophysics e-Prints (ADS) Marshal Space Flight Centre |
| Kennedy Space Centre | Selected Current Aerospace Notice |
| Langley Research Centre | Goddard Space Flight Centre |

NTRS is intended for use by the various research communities targeted by the various report and abstract servers. It is open to all members of the Internet/World Wide Web community. It provides Boolean search facilities.

The user have to single click on the required item to see the abstract and the full text is available in PDF format.

## 24.6 *Conservation database (http:/ / www.wcmc.org.uk/ cis/ index.html)*

This database is maintained by UNEP (United Nation Environment Project) WCMC ( World Conservation Monitoring Centre). It provides information services on conservation and sustainable use of the world's living resources, and helps others to develop information systems of their own.

It is beginning of the process of making this information available through the Internet with this collection of the links, such as Species databases on the world's threatened animals, Plants and trees, Protected Areas, Forest, Marine and National Biodiversity profiles.

### 24.7 *AIRS: Aerometric Information Retrieval Systems (On Atmospheric Pollution) (http:/ / www.epa.gov/ airs/ airs.html)*

In 2001 EPA (Environmental Protection Agency) changed the Aerometric Information Retrieval System (AIRS) to a database that solely related to tracking the compliance of stationary sources of air pollution with EPA regulations. It provides information on Air Pollution, Air facility subsystems, Air quality systems, Air toxics etc.

## 25. Libraries-Virtual Libraries-Digital Libraries (http:/ / www.geocities.com/ ghosh_tbd/ lib.html)

In this section reputed libraries all over the world, different digital libraries and virtual libraries are linked. Among all the libraries following are the most important ones.

### 25.1 *World Libraries on the World Wide Web (http:// www.123world.com/ libraries/ index.html#t)*

It provides ultimate source of authentic and reliable information about 137 of libraries of the world on the net. This list of libraries includes the link of public libraries, research libraries, state libraries, national archives, libraries of different educational institutions, agricultural and technical libraries, business libraries, science libraries, and IMF libraries all over the world. It is arranged in alphabetical order.

### 25.2 *Digital Library of Virginia Tech ( Virginia Polytechnic Institute and State University ): (http:/ / scholar.lib.vt.edu )*

It provides (1) Scholarly Publishing services including

E-journals, Electronic theses & dissertations, news, reports, survey database and Virginia Tech Publications and (2) Library Services and Archives including E-reserves, special collections, manuscripts, rare books, University archives and searching digital library and archives.

**25.3 *Digital Library: University of California : (http://elib.cs.berkeley.edu )***

The University of California, Berkeley Digital Library Project is a part of Digital Libraries Initiative, sponsored by the National Science Foundation and many others. It provides quick access of the collection, overview of the collection, image retrieval by image content, document image analysis and distributed search.

**25.4 *Australian Virtual Engineering Library ( http://avel.edu.au )***

It provides Australian Digital Theses, ENGINE Database from IEAust, SciTech Library Newsletter and Full Text Papers on Biomedicine & Biotechnology, informatics, Nanotechnology, Robotics, Solar Energy, Sustainable Development, Chemical , Civil, Electrical, Environmental and Mechanical and Mining Engineering, Computer Science & I.T. and Engineering Education. This is one of the best site for Engineering and Technology field. It provides full text search facilities. This virtual library is most useful and interesting to the engineering students and academics. The most interesting feature of this library is that users can access and can download their full text resources whatever they digitized. It contains 3,950 documents till date. If the user click on the required item the full text of the document will be available and the user can download the same and can get printout.

**25.5 *Other Virtual Libraries***

All the virtual libraries on Applied Science ands Technology can not be described in a single paper, but among the other virtual libraries following libraries are the most important sources to the academics of Applied Science and Technology.

- Science Virtual Library: http://vlib/Science.html
- Engineering Virtual Library: http://vlib/Engineering.html
- Environmental Virtual Library: http://vlib/Engineering.html

### 26. Earthquake Information (http:// www.geocities.com/ ghosh_svrec/ eqi.html)

In this section following links on earthquake are linked from where the users can get up-to-date information like Earthquake News, Earthquake warning and prediction Research, Earthquake report on different earthquake allover the world.

- US Geological Survey's Earthquake Information
- Earthquake News
- Quakeline Database
- Earthquake Image Information System
- Earthquake warning and Prediction Centre and many other sites on earthquake

### References

Information has been collected from respective websites of the producers which is thankfully acknowledged.

# Index

❑❑❑